MARYLAND
Reflections on 150 Years

THE
DONNING COMPANY
PUBLISHERS

Published on the occasion of the University of Maryland's 150th
Anniversary of its charter date on March 6, 1856

COPYRIGHT © 2006 BY UNIVERSITY OF MARYLAND
First printing February 2006
Second printing September 2006

Office of the Vice President for University Relations
2119 Main Administration Building
University of Maryland
College Park, MD 20742

 Library of Congress Cataloging-in-Publication Data

Maryland : reflections on 150 years.
     p. cm.
 "Published on the occasion of the University of Maryland's 150th Anniversary of its
charter date on March 6, 1856."
  ISBN-13: 978-1-57864-344-8 (hard cover : alk. paper)
  ISBN-10: 1-57864-344-9 (hard cover : alk. paper)
  ISBN-13: 978-1-57864-345-5 (soft cover : alk. paper)
  ISBN-10: 1-57864-345-7 (soft cover : alk. paper)
  1. University of Maryland at College Park--History--Pictorial works.
  LD3231.M702M37 2006
  378.752'51--dc22

                              2005033586

Produced by:
The Donning Company Publishers
184 Business Park Drive, Suite 206
Virginia Beach, VA 23462

Printed in the United States of America at Walsworth Publishing Company

Table of Contents

"The nation that knew no bounds gave birth to an institution that knew no limits."

III by Ira Berlin

THE UNITED STATES was not even a century old when the University of Maryland began to take its present form, but the nation teemed with possibilities. It had already survived longer than any modern republic, demonstrating the superiority of the people's government to that of tyrannical monarchies and haughty aristocracies. Its people had pushed across the continent, and its economy gave them an envious standard of living. Immigrants eager to partake in the nation's bounty poured across its borders. Even as the clouds of Civil War gathered, few Americans doubted that they stood at the cutting edge of history. The future was theirs.

Such an environment promoted innovation. Americans created a host of new institutions, drawing on old forms and giving them a distinctive shape to meet the democratic aspirations of the American people. Some were political, as with parties and their conventions and caucuses. Some were social, as with asylums for the unfortunate, hospitals for the sick, and savings banks for the ambitious. None had a greater impact than the invention of what later became known as the public university. The nation that knew no bounds gave birth to an institution that knew no limits.

Not quickly, however. Scattered across the American landscape, institutions of higher learning took a variety of forms in the 18th and 19th centuries. Some were exclusivist. Others were little more than trade schools. Normal schools educated teachers, and military academies taught soldiers. Many mixed these functions, upon occasion combining them with commitments to scientific scholarship and the liberal arts. All wrestled with old loyalties to church and state and new ideas about academic freedom, and none enjoyed a reliable source of financial support.

Certainly the small agricultural academy carved from Charles Benedict Calvert's Prince George's County plantation in 1856 and championed by that rural gentleman and his slaveholding neighbors offered no solution to multifarious, conflicting demands of practical schooling, humanistic education and professional training. Within the state, the Maryland Agricultural College cast a small shadow, barely large enough to sustain the attention of Maryland's lawmakers. With only a handful of students, no regular curriculum, scant resources and limited public support, it was overshadowed by the professional schools in Baltimore City—predecessors to today's University of Maryland, Baltimore. Even its most enthusiastic supporters could not imagine there was much promise in the school that had sprung up at the railroad crossing in College Park 30 miles to the south.

In 1862, the Morrill Land Grant Act—enacted by the U.S. Congress amid the rampant nationalism of the Civil War—provided resources and assured the state's commitment to the Maryland Agricultural College, which now gained the designation "Land-Grant College." More important, the federal government's endorsement endowed the once-obscure agricultural academy with a mission that reached far beyond its founder's grandest aspiration.

By the early 20th century, Maryland Agricultural College took additional responsibilities through its Extension Service and Experiment Station. But other functions also emerged and carried the college beyond its agricultural roots, as the school added an engineering department, tipped its hat to the liberal arts, encouraged faculty research, cheered student athletes and, in time, admitted women. By the second decade of the 20th century, when the state legislature merged the professional schools at the Baltimore-based University of Maryland with the Maryland State College of Agriculture and gave the former name to both, the College Park campus had come to exemplify the Morrill Act's ideal of the people's university.

More than name now connected the university, the state and the people, and the link between the three grew over the course of the 20th century. The state needed the expertise only the university could supply its citizenry; its citizens saw the university as an avenue for social mobility and personal fulfillment; the university could not exist without the support of both. Their intertwined fate manifested itself in the university's highest aspirations and greatest achievements, as well as its flaws and limitations.

During the 20th century, the university expanded rapidly as the state embraced the nation's struggle against economic depression and then again when the nation went to war against fascism, growing from some 2,000 students in 1935 to more than 10,000 two decades later. The university enjoyed the benefits that accompanied the rise of the activist state: more and better buildings, more professors and more programs. Its growth, moreover, had just begun. Following World War II, thousands of returning veterans, exercising rights bestowed by the GI Bill passed in 1944, poured onto the campus, and their presence, and that of their families, made College Park nothing less than a boom town. New buildings went up fast, but never it seemed fast enough, as new Terps crowded onto the campus—which was now one of the largest public universities in the United States. The generation that had saved the world for democracy now wanted a share of democracy's bounty for themselves and their families.

The democratization of the university followed the democratization of American society in other ways as well. Like the state of Maryland, the university had been strictly segregated by race, isolating students of African descent in a small, underfunded campus on Maryland's Eastern Shore and denying an aspiring attorney, Thurgood Marshall, admission to its law school. However, when the state and the nation turned against segregation, the university embraced racial egalitarianism—cautiously and, perhaps, reluctantly at first but then with enthusiasm. Within a generation of the Supreme Court's decision outlawing racial segregation in public schools, the University of Maryland had been transformed into one of the most diverse campuses in the nation.

Women also gained a new place in the university. The feminist revolution that paralleled the racial revolution of the 1960s deeply affected the University of Maryland, propelling women once defined as "co-eds" toward a place of equality in the classroom, on the faculty and in the administration. Equality, once of little matter to the university community, became an issue of primary concern.

By the late 20th century, the University of Maryland had become a model of the modern research university, committed to the production as well as to the reproduction of knowledge. Internationally recognized faculty, renowned graduate programs, millions of dollars of grants and its "Research One" status spoke to the former. To address the latter—the transfer of knowledge—the university revamped its undergraduate curriculum and introduced dozens of programs to create new connections between undergraduate students and the faculty. Cutting against the impersonality of modern bureaucratic institutions, the University of Maryland—which spent more than a century making the "big store big"—became a national model in "making the big store small."

The university that knows no limits still represents the spirit of the nation that has no bounds. A university committed to scholarship that reaches across the cosmos and teaches color-blind democracy in multicultural classrooms began in a cow pasture of a slaveholding aristocrat. Over the course of 150 years, the University of Maryland has indeed blossomed from its deep roots in Maryland soil.

CHAPTER 1

Our Deep Roots

AMERICA WAS A NATION OF SMALL FARMERS when
Charles Benedict Calvert helped found the Maryland Agricultural
College in 1856. Maryland farmers raised wheat and oats in the
uplands of the Appalachian Region, corn and dairy cattle in the
Piedmont Region stretching north and south of Baltimore, and
tobacco in the Coastal Plain surrounding the Chesapeake Bay.
Calvert and others like him had long dreamed of giving Marylanders
the benefit of the most modern agricultural education.

*In the last half of the 19th century, the Baltimore
and Washington Turnpike (now known as Route 1)
running past the Maryland Agricultural College was
a rutted, narrow, muddy lane, traveled by farmers
in their hay wagons and ox carts and students and
faculty in their carriages.*

Charles Benedict Calvert's financial support was critical to the Maryland Agricultural College's survival in the 1850s. Calvert sold the college a piece of property near College Park for half of its assessed value of $40,000 and loaned the trustees half the purchase price of $20,000. Calvert also was a major stockholder (stock certificate shown left) in the new college. Four of the first 34 students enrolled at the college in 1859 were Calvert's sons.

Oil portrait of Calvert is based upon the image captured by famed Civil War photographer Matthew Brady.

Morrill Hall, the oldest academic building still standing, was erected in 1898 and named in honor of U.S. Senator Justin S. Morrill of Vermont, the author of the Morrill Land Grant Act of 1862. Maryland Agricultural College received its first Morrill Land Grant in 1864.

The first staff of the Agricultural Experiment Station, which conducted research to assist the state's farmers, gathered on the steps of the Rossborough Inn. Henry E. Alvord (center, with long beard) served as the station's first director, from 1888 to 1892, and was also president of the college at the same time. Harry J. Patterson (third from right) put an indelible stamp of professionalism on the station's work during the nearly four decades he served as director, from 1898 to 1937. Patterson also served as president of the Maryland Agricultural College from 1913 to 1917.

CLASS OF 1909

Maryland Agricultural College

Graduates
of Maryland
Agricultural College
between 1903 and 1909
attended school on a campus
that was isolated in time between
the 19th and 20th centuries. Barracks
dating back to before the Civil War stood
side-by-side with modern buildings erected after
the turn of the century.

In the 1910s and 1920s,
the station advanced
the science of livestock
production in a number of
fields, including dairy cattle
management techniques for
control of bovine tuberculosis,
promotion of soybean
production as a cheaper
source of animal feed and
development of an electric
dairy utensil sterilizer.

MARYLAND AGRICULTURAL COLLEGE, like so many land grant colleges in America in the late 19th and early 20th centuries, was first and foremost a military school. The student body was male, and students were addressed as cadets. Until women were admitted to the college in 1916, cadets wore uniforms to class.

Ernest Cory, a 1909 graduate who went on to earn his doctorate and serve as Maryland State Entomologist, recalled in a 1973 interview that "the school was entirely a military school, that is to say, we all wore uniforms, all went out for formations before meals and before going to bed. We marched to class. The man who had charge of the platoon reported who was absent and who was not absent."

As befitting a land grant college, the Maryland Agricultural College educated students for careers on the farm. But the college also had gained a well-deserved reputation for the quality of its engineering and chemistry schools.

No self-respecting mechanical engineering graduate in 1910 would consider leaving home without a sledgehammer, a tool of the trade at a time when steam propulsion ran the manufacturing world. By 1910, the college offered degrees in mechanical, civil and electrical engineering. Maryland Agricultural College engineering graduates could be found in a variety of important positions up and down the East Coast. Herschel Allen, a 1910 graduate, helped design the Chesapeake Bay Bridge near Annapolis, the Potomac River Bridge, the Harbor Tunnel and the Susquehanna River Bridge near Havre de Grace.

Thomas B. Symons, second from right, learned the proper procedures for mixing chemicals in the college's chemistry lab about 1900. Symons, a 1902 graduate, was later dean of the university's College of Agriculture, director of the Cooperative Extension Service from 1914 to 1950, acting president in 1954 and still a member of the Board of Regents at his death in 1970.

The Class of 1906 looked out at the world expectantly when they sat for their junior class photo in April 1905. The majority of the members were residents of Maryland and lived in the barracks or the Administration Building. Some few students from College Park, Riverdale and other nearby farming communities commuted to the school. They were known as "day dodgers."

Pyon Su was the first
Korean student to receive
a degree from an American
college or university. A
member of the Kingdom
of Korea's first diplomatic
delegation to the United
States, Su was admitted to
the Maryland Agricultural
College in the fall of 1887
and graduated with a
bachelor of science degree
in 1891. He was killed
in a train accident in
College Park in October
1891, four months after
graduation.

The student body gathered for a panoramic portrait
sometime in late 1914 or early 1915. Although
uniforms were required at the college until 1916,
about half the students in this informal portrait are in
civilian clothes.

On November 29, 1912, the traditional Thanksgiving Subscription Dance in the main hall of the Administration Buillding was interrupted by whispers of "fire, fire." The 40 couples in attendance rushed out into the night, only to discover that the source of the blaze was in the garret of the Administration Building above them. A brisk southwest wind fanned the blaze, and by midnight, the new Administration Building and the nearby 1859 barracks—home to a majority of the approximately 200 resident students—were skeletal remains. Fears for the college's future proved unfounded, however. According to later accounts, "four days after the fire every student save one reported for duty, resolved to keep the college going." For the next two years, residents of College Park and surrounding communities in Prince George's County opened their homes to cadets while the college built new dormitories.

Charlotte Vaux (right), the first woman to receive a two-year degree from the college in 1918, and Elizabeth Hook, the first woman to take all her classes on campus and receive a four-year degree from the renamed University of Maryland in 1920, are the vanguard of thousands of women students in the next nearly 90 years. Vaux and Hook were admitted in 1916, the year that the General Assembly designated Maryland Agricultural College a full-fledged state institution. The college changed its name to Maryland State College of Agriculture and immediately admitted women students.

Millard Tydings was perhaps ▶ one of the college's most influential early alumni. A 1910 graduate, Tydings was a decorated veteran of World War I and Speaker of the Maryland House of Delegates in 1920 when he introduced legislation to combine Maryland State College and the medical and law schools of the University of Maryland into one university system headquartered in College Park.

The 1920s ushered in the automobile, which made it possible for residents of the growing suburbs of both Washington, D.C., and Baltimore to commute to classes at the university in College Park.

– CHAPTER 2 –

A Legacy of Leadership

||| *by Irwin L. Goldstein*

WHEN I ARRIVED AS A FACULTY MEMBER in 1966, the university was basically a school with an open admissions policy, diversity was not in its dictionary and our athletic teams generated most of the public interest. There were few signs of excellence.

Now, in 2006, parents warn students in high school to work hard to be eligible for admission, and diversity is celebrated as part of our excellence. As a result of our outstanding faculty and staff, we achieve national rankings for programs across the entire university. How did this happen?

My view is that this results from a succession of presidents who had vision and courage to take on challenges and who empowered the university's leadership, faculty and staff to achieve excellence. As dean of the College of Behavioral and Social Sciences, I worked most closely with two presidents: William "Brit" Kirwan and C.D. Mote Jr., known to us as Dan. Each provides wonderful illustrations of what it means to be an outstanding leader.

Shortly after Brit became president, he hosted an event for the campus leadership. Brit opened with a speech saying we would never achieve excellence unless we were the school of choice for Maryland students and that would happen only if we were committed fully to our undergraduates. Brit challenged the deans to work together

and lead the university. From that event, many programs evolved including the living-learning programs known as College Park Scholars, Gemstone and Civicus and numerous interdisciplinary programs that cut across traditional lines. These programs not only gave students exceptional educational opportunities but also changed the culture for undergraduates. Another illustration of Brit's leadership was his commitment to appeal to the U.S. Supreme Court for the right to offer Banneker Scholarships to minorities. The university understood that we were unlikely to prevail, and in fact we did not. Brit's public position, originally espoused by Chancellor John Slaughter, was a statement to the entire community that, for Maryland, diversity as part of excellence is a significant part of our culture.

President Dan Mote arrived at the university and emotionally thrilled the university community with an inaugural address that was a rallying cry for total excellence. Dan charged the university with what it needed to achieve, strongly

stating that a few pillars of excellence do not produce a great institution. Dan made it clear that his vision of excellence included everything we did from academic programs to the arts, from athletic programs to alumni affairs. Dan's vision also included reaching out for partnerships to realize the advantages of our location afforded by the presence of a strong business, research and federal laboratory community. One outcome of this vision is M Square, our research park, and the extraordinary opportunities it will bring.

Another wonderful illustration of Dan's leadership is his concept of Maryland Day—an annual day set aside to share our university with the community. Originally, most staff and faculty did not believe it could work. It is now an event that draws well over 70,000 visitors.

Both Dan and Brit brought to the University of Maryland a vision for achieving excellence; they never wavered from that vision, and they worked tirelessly with university leaders, faculty, students and staff to achieve it. We are still a work in progress. As President Mote says, we still have much more we can achieve as long as we always remember that our focus must be working together to be great at everything we do. At our 150th birthday, I take real pride and pleasure in that thought.

MOST EVERYBODY ON CAMPUS JUST CALLED HIM
"CURLEY." Harry Clifton Byrd dominated the University of
Maryland like no other person in the university's first century of
existence. Born and raised in Crisfield on the state's Eastern Shore,
Byrd came to Maryland Agricultural College in the fall of 1905. He
starred in football, baseball and track before earning his bachelor of
science degree in civil engineering with the class of 1908.

After playing semiprofessional baseball and football, doing
graduate work, covering sports for the old *Washington Star*
and coaching high school football, Byrd returned to
his alma mater in 1912 to coach football for the next
23 years and teach English and history. It was the
beginning of a 42-year career at the university, capped
by 19 years (1935–1954) as president.

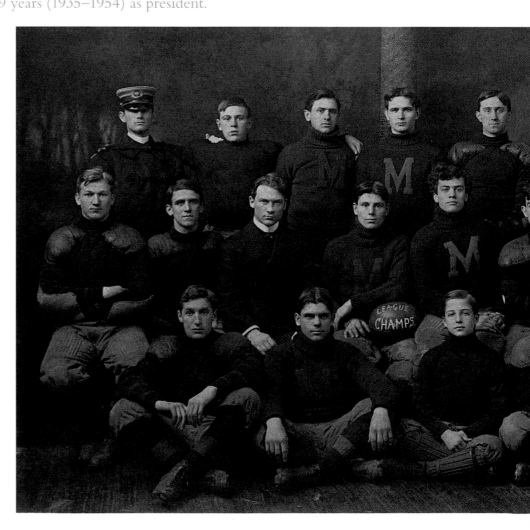

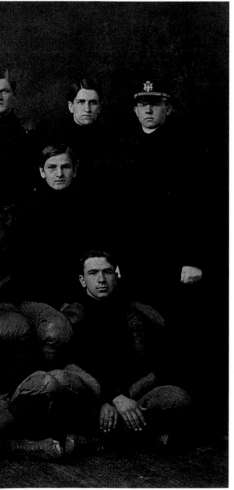

Byrd (to the right of the "League Champs" ball) was one of the stars of the football team from 1905 to 1907. In 1906, the team was 5–3, losing only at Navy, to Georgetown at Griffith Stadium in Washington, D.C., and at Mount Washington.

Harry Clifton Byrd was named acting president of the university in the summer of 1935 and president early the next year. Byrd's official portrait with a set of architectural drawings gripped in his left hand was how many of his contemporaries would remember him. During his administration, the university erected dozens of buildings, including the new Main Administration Building, Symons Hall, the Reckord Armory, Byrd Stadium and the Student Union Building.

Adele H. Stamp was a Maryland native who returned to the state in 1922 to accept the position as the first dean of women at the University of Maryland— and responsibility for the 103 women students at the university at the time. Stamp put her unique mark upon the university during her tenure, which lasted until 1960. She began the campus celebration of May Day in 1923 and was responsible for dozens of campus initiatives, including the creation of Mortar Board, the beginning of women's athletics, the establishment of the code of behavior and the Women's League. Stamp died in 1974 and was honored for her achievements in 1983 when the Student Union was renamed the Adele H. Stamp Student Union.

Long before upheavals at the University of Mississippi and the sit-ins at lunch counters in Greensboro, N.C., Hiram Whittle integrated the University of Maryland without incident, assisted by his attorney, Donald Murray. The university's Board of Regents, at its meeting on Jan. 31, 1951, ordered President Byrd to admit Whittle immediately. Whittle, seen here with roommates at Temporary Dorm One, had completed two and a half years at Morgan State College before applying to Maryland's engineering school. Parren Mitchell, who would go on to a distinguished congressional career, was the first African American student to complete all of his course work on campus and earn a graduate degree at the university in 1952.

Expulsion of Coed From College Backed By Court

Vivian Simpson was an early champion of women's rights at the University of Maryland. The daughter of a Takoma Park grocer, she entered the university with the Class of 1925. In her sophomore year, Simpson and several other women attempted to start a campus chapter of Chi Omega, a national sorority. Simpson hoped to use the sorority to promote women's issues on the predominantly male campus but soon ran afoul of the college administration. When she went to the Washington Post alleging sexual exploitation of coeds by faculty, she was expelled.

Simpson promptly sued the university, won the case in court and then lost on appeal. The episode convinced her to pursue a career in law, which she did with great distinction. Vivian Simpson went on to become Maryland's first woman Secretary of State in 1949 and vice president of the Maryland State Bar Association in 1958. She was named to the Maryland Women's Hall of Fame in 2004.

WILSON ELKINS SUCCEEDED HARRY CLIFTON BYRD as president of the
University of Maryland, guiding the university through the tremendous expansion in
enrollment engendered by the Baby Boom and the unrest that accompanied America's
attempt to draft young men for service in Vietnam. Elkins preached what he called
"quantity of quality" and laid the foundations for the emergence of the modern university.

*President Elkins' commitment fostered higher
academic standards that resulted in Phi Beta Kappa
approving institution of a chapter in 1964, the
university's application having been denied on several
occasions previously. Elkins' Academic Probation
Plan, implemented in 1957, and the restrictions the
university began to impose on admissions led directly to
the rise in academic standards.*

Elkins' biggest challenge was the student unrest that boiled over into sometimes-violent protests at Maryland. In 1970, 1971 and 1972, students blocked Route 1 and forced the governor of Maryland to call out the Maryland National Guard to restore order. Guard platoons outfitted with gas masks fired tear gas canisters to break up the protests and rout students from the campus spaces they occupied, such as in this demonstration by McKeldin Library.

150 Years of Leadership

Benjamin Hallowell, left, served as the first president of the Maryland Agricultural College in 1859. At his death in 1877, a eulogist called him "a great educator in his day. His labors in the field of scientific and literary pursuits have indelibly written his memorial." Hallowell's successors at the helm of the University of Maryland and its predecessors include:

PRESIDENT, MARYLAND AGRICULTURAL COLLEGE

Charles Benedict Calvert, Acting President, 1859–1860
John Work Scott, 1860
John M. Colby, 1860–1861
Henry Onderdonk, 1861–1864
Nicholas B. Worthington, Acting President, 1864–1867
George Washington Custis Lee, 1867 (appointed but never served)
Charles L.C. Minor, 1867–1868
Franklin Buchanan, 1868–1869
Samuel Regester, 1869–1873
Samuel Jones, 1873–1875
William H. Parker, 1875–1882
Augustine J. Smith, 1883–1887
Allen Dodge, Acting President, 1887–1888
Henry E. Alvord, 1888–1892
Richard W. Silvester, 1892–1912
Thomas H. Spence, Acting President, 1912–1913
Harry J. Patterson, 1913–1917★
Albert F. Woods, 1917–1926★

PRESIDENT, UNIVERSITY OF MARYLAND

Raymond A. Pearson, 1926–1935
Harry Clifton Byrd, 1935–1954
Thomas B. Symons, Acting President, 1954
Wilson H. Elkins, 1954–1970

CHANCELLOR, UNIVERSITY OF MARYLAND

Charles E. Bishop, 1970–1974
John W. Dorsey, Acting Chancellor, 1974–1975
Robert L. Gluckstern, 1975–1982
William E. Kirwan, Acting Chancellor, 1982
John B. Slaughter, 1982–1988

PRESIDENT, UNIVERSITY OF MARYLAND

William E. Kirwan, 1988–1998
C.D. Mote Jr., 1998–present

★Institution was known as Maryland State College of Agriculture, 1916–1920.

R. Lee Hornbake was an exemplar of the dynamic breed of postwar educators and administrators who laid the groundwork for the University of Maryland's future educational success. The son of teachers from the Pennsylvania coalfields, Hornbake joined the faculty of the University of Maryland in 1945. During the next 34 years, he built the Department of Industrial Education into one of the nation's finest. He later assumed the newly created position of Vice President for Academic Affairs for Maryland and later for the entire university system. A grateful university named its undergraduate library in his honor in 1980.

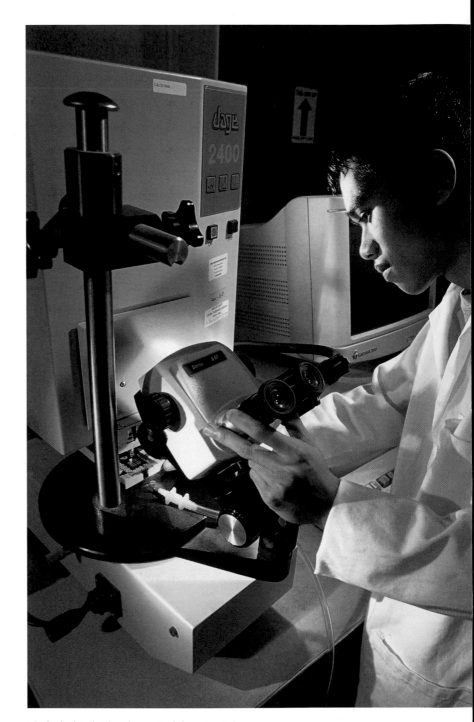

The leadership that has characterized the university's administrative and faculty ranks for the past century-and-a-half has given the university a global reputation, particularly in the sciences. The University of Maryland's biology, engineering, microbiology, computer science and physics departments are often at the cutting edge of 21st-century research.

Even though it had admitted African American students peacefully in the early 1950s, the University of Maryland was not immune from the civil rights unrest that swept America's campuses in the 1960s and 1970s as in this protest on the steps of the Main Administration Building.

Marie Smith Davidson's 30-year-plus career with the university included leadership roles in the administration of three presidents. When she was awarded the President's Medal in 1998, President C.D. Mote Jr. called her "the glue that helps to hold together a large and very complex institution."

Len Bias is shown here shooting over North Carolina's Michael Jordan during a 1983 ACC game that Maryland won, 106–94.

SOMETIMES, AN EVENT CAN TAKE ON TRANSFORMATIONAL
meaning well beyond the ramifications of the event itself. Such was the
case for the University of Maryland with the death of Len Bias. One of
the most talented athletes of his generation, Bias died of a drug overdose
in June 1986, just after being selected the number two pick in the National
Basketball Association draft. The death of Len Bias was a watershed event
in the history of the modern university. Chancellor John Slaughter and the
Board of Regents embarked upon the process of rethinking institutional
standards that would become the basis for dramatic improvement in
university academics and athletics.

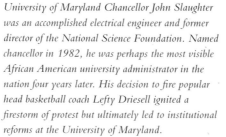

*An agenda for diversity—
based upon leadership
that began with Robert
Gluckstern to current
president C.D. Mote—
established significant
programs to build diversity.*

*University of Maryland Chancellor John Slaughter
was an accomplished electrical engineer and former
director of the National Science Foundation. Named
chancellor in 1982, he was perhaps the most visible
African American university administrator in the
nation four years later. His decision to fire popular
head basketball coach Lefty Driesell ignited a
firestorm of protest but ultimately led to institutional
reforms at the University of Maryland.*

The ruby focus of a laser is a symbol of the success by leaders of the university in attracting research investment. Located in the heart of the Baltimore-Washington corridor and its proliferation of federal agencies and private laboratories, the university is increasingly a research partner for a long and growing list of federal, state and private sector organizations.

◀ The Omicron Delta Kappa fountain at the center of McKeldin Mall is a reminder of the role that leadership plays throughout the academic community. Established as the leadership fraternity on campus in 1927, Omicron Delta Kappa and its alumni donated the 16-ft.-by-250-ft. fountain to the university when the mall was reconstructed in 1990.

William Kirwan (left) and C.D. Mote Jr. meet at the President's Residence in 1998, shortly after the regents announced that Mote would replace Kirwan as president of the university. Kirwan's presidency from 1989 to 1998 was a time of dramatic improvement of undergraduate education. Mote quickly laid the foundation for greatness in academics, athletics, the arts and economic development in the 21st century. He continues to push the university to new levels of achievement.

– CHAPTER 3 –

Faculty at the Forefront

||| *by J. Robert Dorfman*

THE MOST VALUED AND RESPECTED FACULTY MEMBERS are those who have open, creative minds; the ability to communicate the importance of their work to others, particularly students; and the ability to inspire their students to try new ideas, or pursue new paths.

Such faculty members and their students provide the energy that drives the creative life of the university. This energy has its sources in questions the faculty and students set for themselves and for each other and in the creative power of individuals and groups of collaborators to answer these questions. As notable examples, I think of Ken Holum and his students who are very actively involved in the archaeological excavations in Caesarea Maritima on the Mediterranean coast in Israel or Jim Yorke and his students who use mathematical methods developed for the theory of chaos to investigate ways to improve weather prediction and the analysis of the human genome.

Inquiries, such as those mentioned above, may be in any of a wide range of scholarly, scientific, practical, artistic or societal fields. The sole overall criteria should be that the work is painstaking and of a high standard and that the topics studied or worked upon be profound enough to engage the minds and talents of members of the university community. The University of Maryland has earned its reputation as just

such an intellectually exciting and creative community—deservedly counted among the best public universities in the United States.

From my first days as an undergraduate student, academic life held appeal because of the focus on fundamental issues of science, in particular, and for the honesty and rigor demanded of scientific research. My own long-standing affiliation with Maryland began in 1964 as a young assistant professor in the Department of Physics, then under the leadership of John Toll, who was a formidable force in laying the foundation for the department where I still teach. My work in the field of mathematical statistical mechanics was conducted in the Institute for Fluid Dynamics and Applied Mathematics (now the Institute for Physical Science and Technology).

The university was, and remains today, very supportive of its faculty. Of equal importance to me was the opportunity to be a part of a public university with a distinguished faculty in many areas, not only in the sciences. Over the years, I have

taken courses taught by colleagues in art history, Hebrew studies, Jewish studies and mathematics.

At mid-career, it seemed time for me to assume some personal responsibility for helping the university grow and improve. I was fortunate to serve in a number of roles—director, dean and, ultimately, vice president for academic affairs and provost during the presidency of Brit Kirwan. Although my time in the administration was fruitful, I was quite happy to return to my life as a faculty member. As a researcher, one of the most rewarding experiences is the feeling that comes when one has made some progress in resolving the issue being studied or found a new and productive line of inquiry.

As a teacher and mentor, there is nothing that compares to the pleasure of seeing students grasp difficult concepts for the first time or make a dramatic discovery in their own research work. Such achievements continue to drive me today as they did 40-plus years ago when I decided to make the University of Maryland my home.

Distinguished
UNIVERSITY PROFESSORS

The designation of Distinguished University Professor is the highest academic honor given by the university, in recognition of faculty who are considered leaders in their fields of study. The program was formalized in 1995 by then-president, William E. Kirwan. As of fall 2005, 54 members of the faculty have been awarded the distinction.

MICHAEL F. A'HEARN (2000)
Department of Astronomy
A'Hearn is regarded as the leading international authority on the physical composition and chemical properties of comets and as perhaps the foremost intellectual leader in the field of cometary physics. He is the lead scientist for NASA's Deep Impact project, successfully launched in 2005.

MILLARD ALEXANDER (1999)
Department of Chemistry and Biochemistry/Institute for Physical Science and Technology
Alexander is recognized around the world for his work in molecular physics, including his theoretical study of inelastic and reactive molecular collisions, including those involving free radicals.

STUART S. ANTMAN (2001)
Department of Mathematics
Antman is one of the leading experts in the field of mathematical elasticity, to which he has made outstanding contributions during the past 35 years. He is internationally renowned for his analyses of nonlinear problems of mechanics, especially the mechanics of solids, and for nonlinear analysis of differential equations.

IVO BABUSKA (1995) §
Department of Mathematics/Institute for Physical Science and Technology
Babuska has played an essential role in advancing research in the field of general and computational mechanics. Both mathematicians and engineers have embraced his contributions to the finite element method. He is also a member of the National Academy of Engineering.

† no longer at university
§ emeritus
★ deceased

SINCE ITS FORMATION AS THE MARYLAND Agricultural College in 1856, the university has attracted some of the best and the brightest minds in mathematics and the sciences to its faculty.

William D. Phillips, who achieved his Nobel Prize in 1997 for his work at the nearby National Institute of Standards and Technology (NIST) in atomic physics, is the first Nobel Laureate appointed to a full faculty position in the long history of the university. Now Distinguished University Professor in the Department of Physics, he specializes in molecular, atomic and optical physics.

Sylvester James Gates, holder of the John S. Toll Endowed Professorship in Physics, also is the first African American to hold an endowed chair at a major research institution in the United States. Known for his groundbreaking work in the areas of superstring theory, supersymmetry and supergravity, Gates co-authored the book Superspace or 1001 Lessons in Supersymmetry, *which two decades later remains the standard in the field. His work is considered a successor to Einstein's groundbreaking research.*

Statistical properties of nanostructures is one of the many research fields investigated by Ellen Williams, Distinguished University Professor, Physics. With her establishment of the Williams Lab, she has provided pioneering leadership for the university's initiatives in nanoscience and biophysics. Coupling her research interests with a heavy teaching load, Williams embodies the tradition of excellence in mathematics and sciences for which the university is known.

Distinguished
UNIVERSITY PROFESSORS

RITA COLWELL (2004) §
Institute for Computer Studies (UMIACS)
Colwell is internationally renowned for her work in microbial biodiversity and marine and estuarine microbial ecology. A former president of the University of Maryland Biotechnology Institute, she has also served as president of the American Association for the Advancement of Science and as director of the National Science Foundation.

SANKAR DAS SARMA (1995)
Department of Physics
As a physics researcher, Das Sarma has centered his studies on condensed matter physics, materials science and statistical mechanics. The Condensed Matter Theory Group he leads has published more than 60 scholarly papers.

THEODOR DIENER (1999) §
Department of Cell Biology and Molecular Genetics/ Center for Agricultural Biotechnology
Diener's extensive studies on plant and pathogen interaction have produced strategies for enhancing plant protection. He is a recipient of the National Medal of Science.

DAVID C. DRISKELL (1995) §
Department of Art
A leading authority on African American art and an established artist in his own right, Driskell has been a mentor to artists, collectors and historians. His exhibition, "Narratives of African American Art and Identity: The David C. Driskell Collection," showcased the work of 61 African American artists.

RICHARD A. ETLIN (2000)
Department of Architecture
Etlin is one of the most distinguished scholars in the field of architectural history and related humanistic disciplines. His books and numerous scholarly papers and articles exemplify breadth of interest, high standards of scholarship, and lucid writing. Accolades for his work include the Best New Book in Architecture and Planning Award from the American Association of Publishers, the Alice Davis Hitchcock Book Award for the most distinguished work of scholarship in the history of architecture, and an AIA International Architecture Book Award.

LIFE SCIENCES AND HEALTH INITIATIVES continue to create news at the University of Maryland. In 2005, the university created the Fischell Department of Bioengineering by assembling faculty from engineering, health and human performance, and other campus units, by creating split appointments across colleges and the University System of Maryland (USM) institutions, and by recruiting new faculty. When the Ph.D. program in bioengineering was established in 2002, it attracted the participation of 51 faculty members from 22 university and USM departments and institutions.

The University of Maryland is also taking a leading role in researching avian influenza, the virus that many public health officials fear could spur a worldwide pandemic. Assistant Professor Daniel Perez, an avian influenza researcher, has been named to head a new, far-reaching national research and education project, funded with a $5 million grant from the U.S. Department of Agriculture. It is the largest grant ever given by the USDA to study a single animal disease or health threat. Researchers and extension specialists from 17 states are involved in the Maryland-led initiative.

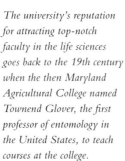

The university's reputation for attracting top-notch faculty in the life sciences goes back to the 19th century when the then Maryland Agricultural College named Townend Glover, the first professor of entomology in the United States, to teach courses at the college.

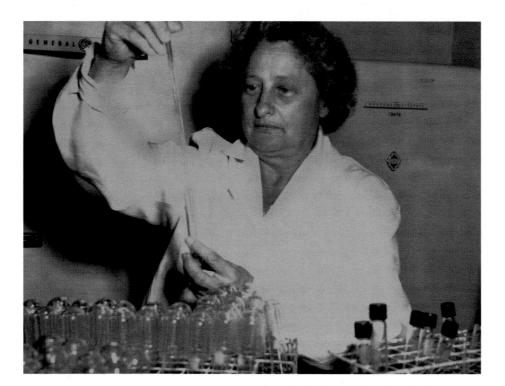

Mary S. Shorb, a research professor in the Department of Poultry Science from 1949 to 1972, was another who advanced knowledge of the life sciences during her tenure at the university. Shorb, who also worked part time for the National Institutes of Health in nearby Bethesda and frequently lectured at Oxford University, is credited with leading the team that discovered Vitamin B12.

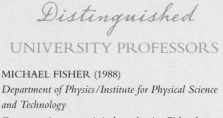

Distinguished
UNIVERSITY PROFESSORS

MICHAEL FISHER (1988)
Department of Physics/Institute for Physical Science and Technology
Concentrating on statistical mechanics, Fisher has been recognized for his seminal contributions to the field by receiving the prestigious Wolf Prize. He is also a Fellow of the American Academy of Arts and Sciences.

MARK I. FREIDLIN (2000)
Department of Mathematics
Freidlin is an internationally prominent mathematician who has made and continues to make seminal contributions to the field of dynamical systems theory. He has developed precise models of how small random perturbations affect dynamical systems and has also created rigorous and productive models that have been applied to problems in biophysics, oceanography and meteorology.

ELISABETH GANTT (1997)
Department of Microbiology
A leading researcher in the field of plant biology, Gantt's pioneering studies include research on photosynthesis and algae, stimulating work in a number of important problems in biology and biophysics. She is also a member of the National Academy of Sciences.

BRUCE L. GARDNER (1995)
Department of Agricultural and Resource Economics
A specialist in agricultural and natural resources policy, Gardner has investigated farm policies in the United States with a focus on governmental regulation of food prices.

JAMES GILBERT (1999)
Department of History
Gilbert continues to gain recognition for his studies exploring the intersection of American culture and religion in the 19th and 20th centuries. He has authored several monographs and books including *Perfect Cities: Chicago's Utopias in the 1890s*, selected by *The New York Times* as one of its "Notable Books of 1991." He is also founder of the Center for Historical Studies at the University of Maryland.

Distinguished
UNIVERSITY PROFESSORS

GEORGE GLOECKLER (1998)
Department of Physics/Institute for Physical Science and Technology
One of the world's leading researchers in space radiation, Gloeckler has been recognized for his development of instruments used on Earth's satellites and space probes. He is also a member of the National Academy of Sciences.

TED ROBERT GURR (1995) §
Department of Government and Politics
As an expert in global conflict affairs, Gurr has conducted groundbreaking research on civil conflict and political violence, identifying ethno-political conflicts around the world.

LOUIS R. HARLAN (1984) §
Department of History
A former president of the Organization of American Historians, American Historical Association, and Southern Historical Association, Harlan holds a Pulitzer Prize, two Bancroft Prizes, and the Beveridge Prize. One of the nation's most renowned and respected historians, he was awarded the Pulitzer Prize in Biography or Autobiography in 1984 for *Booker T. Washington: The Wizard of Tuskegee.*

WILLIAM HODOS (2004) §
Department of Psychology
Hodos has virtually defined the fields of comparative psychology and comparative neurobiology. Most recently, he published the leading textbook on comparative vertebrate anatomy. Finally, Hodos pioneered and populated the toolbox of experimental techniques used by comparative psychologists, such as the methodology for studying pain and its opposite, motivation, to obtain a reward.

RICHARD E. JUST (1995)
Department of Agricultural and Resource Economics
An authority on the political economy of transboundary water issues, Just's recommendations on the issue of water rights have been influential in the historic peace treaty negotiated between Jordan and Israel.

UNIVERSITY PRESIDENT C.D. MOTE JR. noted in his 2005 State of the Campus address that the Deep Impact Project, which targeted the Comet Tempel 1 in the biggest July 4th fireworks display since the nation's Bicentennial in 1976, was "an impact felt around this world as well as out of it."

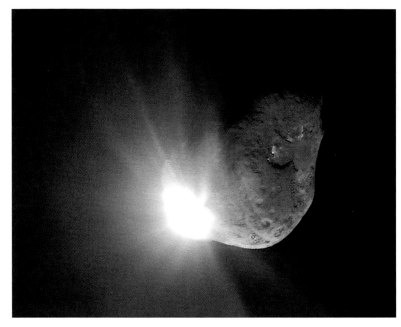

When NASA's Deep Impact probe collided with Tempel 1, a bright flash was created, which rapidly expanded above the surface of the comet.

Chaos theory is another field in which the university has established a claim of solid leadership. James Yorke (pictured below), Distinguished University Professor, Mathematics and Physics, is a founder and leader of the field of chaos theory. The winner of the 2003 Japan Prize, Yorke coined the use of the term "chaos" in 1975 for the mathematical study of nonlinear dynamic systems. Yorke is currently involved in research projects that range from chaos theory and weather prediction to genome research to the population dynamics of the HIV/AIDS epidemic.

Led by Michael A'Hearn, Deep Impact, a $312 million mission, successfully launched a projectile deep into the nucleus of a passing comet to uncover secrets about the origin of the solar system. A'Hearn, a Distinguished University Professor, Astronomy, is regarded as the leading international authority on the physical composition and chemical properties of comets and perhaps the foremost intellectual leader in the field of cometary physics. He is shown here with co-investigator Lucy McFadden, Professor of Astronomy.

Distinguished
UNIVERSITY PROFESSORS

EUGENIA E. KALNAY (2001)
Department of Meteorology/Institute for Physical Science and Technology
Eugenia Kalnay is a world-class scientist of great distinction who has had a major impact on the field of weather forecasting. She has been, for several decades now, the primary intellectual leader in the United States in the development of new approaches for and applications of numerical weather prediction. She is also a member of the National Academy of Engineering.

ARIE W. KRUGLANSKI (2003)
Department of Psychology
Kruglanski's ability to grasp and create the "big picture" for the study of human knowledge and human judgment has made him one of the 25 most frequently cited social psychologists in the world.

HOWARD B. LASNIK (2003)
Department of Linguistics
Lasnik is one of the most productive and influential figures in the study of language over the past quarter-century. He has made a number of major contributions to the recent advances in our rapidly deepening understanding of the structure of language and its processing demands upon speakers.

JERROLD LEVINSON (2004)
Department of Philosophy
Levinson is a world-famous philosopher of the arts and aesthetics, including music and literature. A distinguished group of international experts consider him to be one of the world's outstanding philosophers of art.

GEORGE H. LORIMER (2000)
Department of Chemistry and Biochemistry
Lorimer is one of the world's most eminent biochemists. His work has made seminal contributions to enzymology and, more recently, to the study of protein folding. His research combines a sharp perception of what are the next most important questions to be asked and the creative use of modern technology in seeking answers to these questions. He is also a member of the National Academy of Sciences.

Distinguished
UNIVERSITY PROFESSORS

SERGEI P. NOVIKOV (1997)
Department of Mathematics/Institute for Physical Science and Technology
Novikov became one of just eight mathematicians to have received both the Fields Medal and the Wolf Prize when he was awarded the Wolf Prize in 2005. He is regarded as one of the world's greatest topologists, studying the graphic delineation of man-made features that show their relative positions and elevations. He is also a member of the National Academy of Sciences.

MANCUR OLSON (1980) *
Department of Economics
A leading pioneer in economics, Olson was recognized as one of a selected few scholars responsible for changing the field, ensuring that politics became an essential part of economic thinking. In the international arena, he provided economic guidance to more than 30 former communist countries.

EDWARD OTT (1995)
Department of Electrical Engineering/Department of Physics
Ott is noted for his involvement in the development of chaos theory and the measurement and control of chaotic systems. His ideas have revolutionized communication systems.

JOSÉ EMILIO PACHÉCO (1995)
Department of Spanish and Portuguese Languages
Renowned poet, novelist, translator and critic, Pachéco has received awards such as the National Prize for Literature from the president of Mexico and the National Prize for Journalism.

WILLIAM D. PHILLIPS (2001)
Department of Physics/Institute for Physical Science and Technology
Philips shared the 1997 Nobel Prize in Physics "for the development of methods to cool and trap atoms with lasers." He is considered one of the greatest experimental physicists of our age, transforming the field in which he works. He is the leading researcher of ultra-low temperature atomic physics in the world.

Juan Ramón Jiménez at the University of Puerto Rico.

LIBERAL ARTS have never taken second place to the sciences at the university when it comes to the accomplishments of faculty. Nobel Prize winner Juan Ramón Jiménez was a professor of modern languages in the 1950s, and Gordon Prange became a best-selling author in the 1980s with his histories of the Pacific theater during World War II.

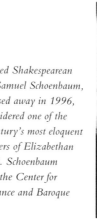
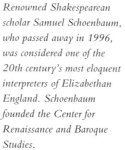

Renowned Shakespearean scholar Samuel Schoenbaum, who passed away in 1996, was considered one of the 20th century's most eloquent interpreters of Elizabethan England. Schoenbaum founded the Center for Renaissance and Baroque Studies.

Ira Berlin (pictured above), Distinguished University Professor, History, is an internationally recognized scholar on American history in the 19th century, particularly on Southern and African-American life. Berlin has become the pre-eminent scholar in America on the subject of slavery.

An accomplished administrator as well as a celebrated historical scholar, Berlin has served as the university's dean for undergraduate studies where he established innovative living and learning programs, beginning with College Park Scholars, which became models for academic programs elsewhere in North America.

Distinguished
UNIVERSITY PROFESSORS

STANLEY PLUMLY (1998)
Department of English
Admired as a poet and a critic, Plumly is the author of seven award-winning volumes of poetry, praised for their elegance of style. He has received a Guggenheim Foundation Fellowship and the National Book Critics Circle Award.

HARRIET B. PRESSER (1998)
Department of Sociology
An authority on shift work, Presser has conducted various studies on social demography, fertility and interrelationships among gender, work and family, specifically focusing on issues such as unemployment in the United States. Her work is a rare blend of rigorous scholarship with immediate and crucial policy implications.

RAMAMOORTHY RAMESH (2003) †
Department of Materials Science and Engineering/ Department of Physics
With experience in industry research and development as well as academia, Ramesh quickly developed an international reputation for his work in the science and technology of complex materials, including thin film growth and materials physics of complex oxides leading to new understanding of the properties of material physics at nano-scale levels.

GEORGE RITZER (2001)
Department of Sociology
Ritzer is one of the most visible and respected sociologists specializing in social theory and its application to everyday realms of economics and consumption. His scholarship has not only had a significant impact on the discipline of sociology but has also gained him the reputation as a public intellectual of major significance.

AZRIEL ROSENFELD (1995) ★
Director, Center for Automation Research
Rosenfeld, a researcher in the field of automated vision/sensing systems, concentrated on computer vision, enabling computers "to see" by recognizing and analyzing images.

Distinguished
UNIVERSITY PROFESSORS

ROALD Z. SAGDEEV (1990)
Department of Physics and Director, East-West Space Science Center
One of the world's leading physicists, Sagdeev is renowned for his work on nonlinear space plasmas. He has sparked dynamic advances in space exploration, such as the satellite encounter with Comet Halley. He is also a member of the National Academy of Sciences.

THOMAS C. SCHELLING (1990) §
School of Public Policy/Department of Economics
As an economist at the top of his field of applied game theory, Schelling was co-recipient of the 2005 Nobel Prize in Economics. He has also applied game theory in designing environmental regulations, setting criminal penalties and reforming insurance markets.

ALLEN SCHICK (2001)
School of Public Policy
As a scholar, Schick is widely regarded as one of the most important contributors to the study of public budgeting and finance in the past generation. His more than a dozen books include the profoundly influential *The Federal Budget: Politics, Policy, and Process, The Spirit of Reform* and *The Politics of the Budgetary Process.* In 1989 he was awarded the Waldo Prize by the American Society for Public Administration for lifetime contributions to the literature of public administration.

SAMUEL SCHOENBAUM (1980) ★
Department of English
Renowned in renaissance and baroque studies and the author of several biographies on William Shakespeare, Schoenbaum's numerous awards include two Guggenheim Fellowships.

JAN V. SENGERS (1999) §
Institute for Physical Science and Technology/ Department of Chemical Engineering
Among Sengers' achievements are theoretical and experimental advancements in thermodynamic and transport properties of fluids. He is a Fellow of the American Physical Society.

WITH MORE THAN A CENTURY of accomplishments, faculty of the A. James Clark School of Engineering and the Glenn L. Martin Institute of Technology have made engineering one of the university's consistently brightest disciplines.

The A. James Clark School of Engineering boasts four institutes, more than 130 labs and 23 research centers in which faculty and students examine everything from the physics of turbulence to environmental energy.

The Innovation Hall of Fame, in the Jeong H. Kim Engineering Building, honors engineers for their advancements. Among the faculty luminaries are Hung C. Lin, an early pioneer in the creation of semiconductor devices and integrated circuits; John E. Younger, an innovator in the rapidly evolving technology of all-metal airplanes; and Joseph Weber (pictured at right), who conceived of the idea of coherent microwave emissions, which led to the development of the laser.

S. Sidney Steinberg (shown at left), professor and head of the civil engineering department during the 1930s, was dean of the College of Engineering from 1936 to 1956. As dean, his door was always open to the college's primarily undergraduate enrollment.

SOCIAL SCIENCES AND PUBLIC POLICY faculty
have compiled a record of innovative research and solid
teaching credentials that is the envy of many in the
academic and government communities.

*Distinguished University
Professor Emeritus Thomas
C. Schelling won the 2005
Nobel Memorial Prize in
Economics for his work in
game theory analysis and
has published influential
works in areas ranging
from nuclear proliferation
and arms control to racial
segregation. His work on
nuclear deterrence helped
shape Cold War strategies.*

Harriet Presser, Distinguished University Professor, Sociology, is the founding director of what is now the Maryland Population Research Center. Named a Fellow of the American Association for the Advancement of Science in 2002, Presser studies population and family policy issues from a national and international perspective and teaches courses in population, gender and social demography.

Benjamin Barber is one of the premier democratic theorists of the past quarter-century. A Distinguished University Professor, he enjoys international renown as one of the globe's leading scholars in the field of democratic participation and the cultivation of civic life. His book, Jihad vs. McWorld, *rose to the top of the bestseller list after 9/11. The current University System of Maryland Wilson H. Elkins Professor, Barber is one of the first scholars to identify the increasing economic and cultural integration we now call globalization.*

– CHAPTER 4 –

Changing Times:
Student Life, Past & Present

III *by Leonard J. Elmore*

AUTUMN 1970, MY FRESHMAN YEAR, was both ideal and surreal. Awed by the expanse of the campus, this city boy from New York attempted to navigate the maze of the mall and the complexity of registration at the Armory. My anxiety was reflected in the eyes of my freshmen classmates as they self-consciously tiptoed from class hall to class hall trying to find their correct room.

That year, Ellicott Hall was my home where I encountered a decidedly unmatched mix of floor mates. Present were the obligatory "long-haired freaks" (come to think of it, my Afro was becoming kind of long and unshaped), replete with patchwork jeans and bare feet. They co-existed with military veterans, several of whom had seen action in Vietnam. All now were cashing in on the promise of the GI Bill's assistance. I recall huddling in dorm rooms previewing the latest rock group albums. To discuss the war, politics and race relations and to listen to the music of our generation was a huge part of my education.

Campus upheaval shattered this idyllic bliss as demonstrations against the U.S.-led invasion into Cambodia continued through the fall. The South Chapel lawn offered a seemingly never-ending clash between state troopers and National Guardsmen and

demonstrators, some of whom wore wildly colored bandanas that doubled as slingshots to fling fired tear gas canisters back to authorities. Suddenly, the wind changed direction and we were gassed. Call it collateral damage, I guess. The exclamation point came when a plane, flying low over the campus presented a taped curfew message over its loud speaker, "This is [Adjutant] General Warfield," but sounded to this scared freshman as, "This is general warfare."

The South Chapel lawn was the scene of another irony. While playing softball, we were witness to 15 or more speeding police cars, sirens wailing. Segregationist George Wallace had been shot at the Laurel Shopping Center. Less than a decade before, lunch counters were segregated

along the Route 1 corridor. Yet, here in 1972, cheers erupted from blacks and whites alike at the news.

As troubling as the early '70s were in many ways, it was also a time of great joy, personally. Basketball was my fulcrum. With Tom McMillen and my other teammates, we brought Maryland basketball to national prominence under the spotlight with 14,500 adoring fans each night in Cole Field House. We won the 1972 NIT, made the 1973 NCAA Elite Eight and, ranked No. 4 in the nation, lost in overtime to No. 1 and eventual national champions, N.C. State, in the 1974 ACC Tournament final, called by most ACC fans the greatest game ever played.

But even that loss couldn't conjure regrets in my basketball life. Academics were

a different story. A bright but immature student, my lack of focus forced me to attend class for three summers beyond my graduation class of 1974, even while I had begun my career as a professional basketball player. Perhaps that is why now I am so committed to student-athletes and education.

My reflections of Maryland are in juxtaposition—a time of growth and maturity marked by startling events. Being a Terp offered me a true love of life in a way I could never have learned in the off-campus world of the early '70s.

FOR STUDENTS, THE MORE THINGS CHANGE, the more they remain the same. Leaving home, high school and family for life at Maryland is a rite of passage that generations of freshmen have experienced—and cherished. College life creates lifelong friendships cemented in the shared memories of all-night gabfests, cramming for finals, leaving offerings for Testudo and cheering the Terps on to another hard-fought victory.

From the turn of the 19th century to the 1990s, Maryland students looked to a handbook, often titled the M Book, for guidance.

The music changes, but the chance to have a good time at the fraternity dance transcends generations. This group of revelers gathered at the Delta Mu Fraternity's spring dance at the Roosevelt Hotel in Washington, D.C., in 1927. They likely shocked their adult chaperones by doing the Charleston, the latest dance craze.

Dorm life at the Maryland Agricultural College in the early 20th century was probably not a lot different than it is today. Male students decorated their rooms with poster pin-ups, and it was never too difficult to find four or five residents to gather for a late-night bull session.

It was tough being a member of the Maryland Agricultural College's football squad in 1892, the first year the school fielded a varsity team. The squad's 0–3 record included a 62–0 drubbing by Johns Hopkins and a 16–0 loss to Episcopal High School. The next year, MAC claimed the D.C. Championship with a 6–0 record, beginning the school's reputation as a gridiron powerhouse.

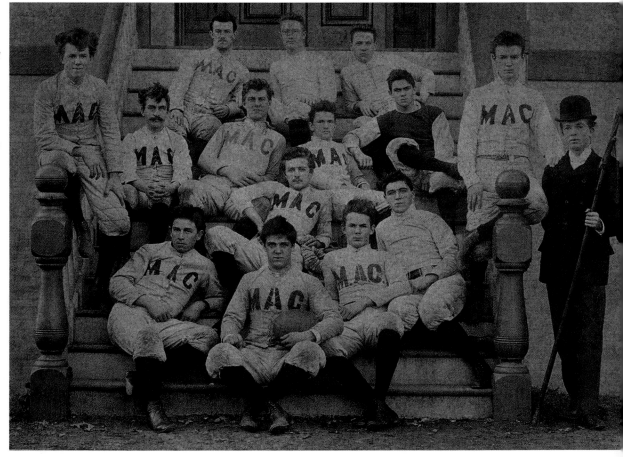

UNDERGRADS, FACULTY, ALUMNI and state residents alike find common ground in talking about how the Terps did last Saturday in the big game. It doesn't matter whether the sport is played by men or women, whether it's a key ACC struggle against Duke at Cole or a women's lacrosse practice on campus in the pouring rain, somebody plays—and somebody cares.

MARYLAND • NORTH CAROLINA

HER MAJESTY, QUEEN ELIZABETH II

SATURDAY, OCTOBER 19, 1957 • BYRD STADIUM • COLLEGE PARK, MARYLAND

Queen but four years, Elizabeth II made her first state visit to the former colonies in 1957. The Queen's staff arranged for her and Prince Philip to attend the Maryland-North Carolina football game at Byrd Stadium on October 19. Maryland Governor Theodore McKeldin and University of Maryland President Wilson Elkins hosted the royal couple in a box on the 50-yard line. The 43,000 Terrapin fans in attendance cheered both the Queen and the underdog home team, who defeated the Tar Heels 21–7.

Maryland came to prominence in the early 1930s for its intercollegiate boxing teams. Under renowned coach Col. Harvey "Heinie" Miller, the university was a power in boxing throughout the Great Depression, World War II and after. One of Miller's greatest boxers was two-time national champion Benny Alperstein (seen here TKOing Harry Rising of Army in 1939).

Terps quarterback Jack
Scarbath scored the first
touchdown against Navy on
Sept. 30, 1950, opening day
in the new Byrd Stadium.
The capacity crowd of
43,836 saw Maryland rout
the rival Middies, 35–21.

The first varsity athletes
on campus, the Maryland
Agricultural College baseball
team, in this early 1890s
photo, played against such
foes as Navy and Johns
Hopkins. MAC won its first
baseball championship in
1898.

Dean of Women Adele Stamp instituted May Day in 1923 to honor and celebrate women and their achievements. The May Day festivities included the crowning of the May Queen and her court, a May Pole Dance and the presentation of a themed play by the junior women. May Day festivities were celebrated annually for almost four decades—the last in 1961.

Paula Gwynn, a freshman radio, television and film major, steps forward to acknowledge the cheers of the crowd at the Miss Black Unity Pageant on Nov. 23, 1985. The annual event was a source of African American pride for more than two decades, beginning in 1977.

The outdoor stage at the Nyumburu Cultural Center is a popular gathering spot. ▶

By 1981–1982, when the Terps went 25–7 and reached the NCAA Final Four, women's basketball at Maryland had come of age. Under Coach Chris Weller from 1975 to 2002, the women's team won 499 games and an unprecedented eight ACC championships.

OVER THE PAST SEVERAL DECADES, no sport brought Maryland more national acclaim than basketball. A member of the tough Atlantic Coast Conference for more than a half-century, Maryland competes against such powerhouses as Duke, North Carolina and Wake Forest.

The 1927 women's basketball team played an intramural schedule that was only four years old at the time.

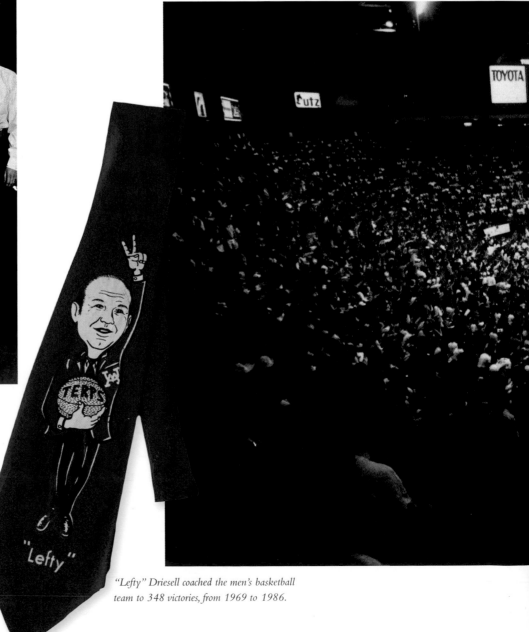

"Lefty" Driesell coached the men's basketball team to 348 victories, from 1969 to 1986.

Future All-Americans Len Elmore and Tom McMillen were members of the 1970–1971 freshmen men's basketball team that sportswriters and coaches ranked No. 1 in the nation. They and John Lucas were three consensus All-Americans on the 1973–1974 squad that may have been the best basketball team ever assembled at Maryland. At a time when only one conference team was invited to the NCAA Tournament, Maryland lost its chance to go to the Big Dance when it was beaten in a heartbreaker by North Carolina State in the finals of the ACC Championship.

In his senior year, Len Elmore earned All-American honors and helped lead Maryland to one of its best seasons ever. His 412 rebounds in 1974 are still a school record. Following a 10-year career in professional basketball, Elmore earned his law degree from Harvard Law School in 1987.

The University of Maryland women's basketball team set an ACC attendance record by selling out Cole Field House in 1992.

Inside, the Armory offered a different picture of campus life during certain times of the year. Registration brought out what often appeared to be chaos as hordes of students tried to create a schedule that minimized early morning classes.

Students frequently comment upon the beauty of the campus, as this shot of the Armory framed by cherry blossoms attests.

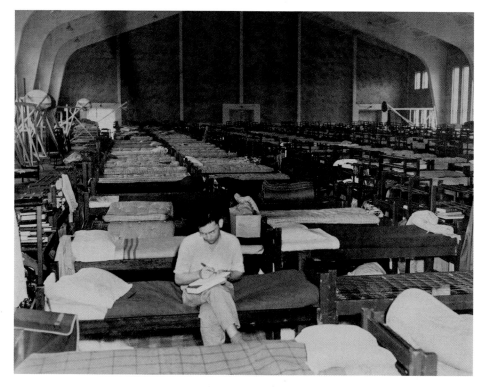

The Armory served yet another purpose in 1946 and 1947 when thousands of veterans enrolled at the university to earn an education and take advantage of the GI Bill of Rights, which helped pay tuition and living expenses. Accustomed to living in barracks, the returning veterans had little problem adjusting to sleeping on bunk beds in the cavernous Armory.

Cole Field House is perhaps best known to generations of Maryland fans as the home court of the Terps from 1955 to 2002. Many will remember other rituals held within those walls—the joy of their commencement ceremony or, less fondly, that final exam. The venerable field house was also the site for an Elvis Presley concert in 1974.

At 7 a.m. each Thursday, AFROTC students gather for reveille in front of the Armory.

From the 1920s to the 1960s, freshmen were required to wear their beanies until the freshman-sophomore tug-of-war in the spring.

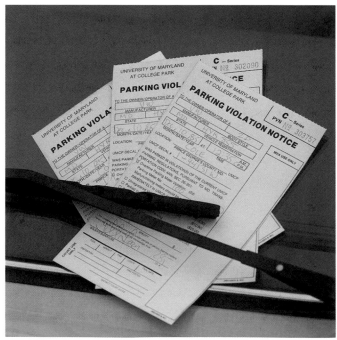

What student with a car hasn't received at least one parking ticket during his or her years at the university?

Come the first nice early spring day, the stands of Byrd Stadium fill with youthful sun worshippers working on their tans. Byrd Beach has been a tradition at Maryland since the stadium first opened in 1950.

Over the decades, commuter students spent countless hours in the Commuter Lounge at Stamp Student Union.

Turtle races were a popular tradition in the '50s and '60s, with sponsors ranging from fraternities to residence halls.

This alumnus proudly proclaims allegiance to the University of Maryland.

The men's national championship basketball team prepares to break from the huddle just prior to a game during the magical 2002 season. After chasing the dream of a national championship since the 1939 onset of the NCAA tournament, Maryland prevailed.

The 1953 Terrapins football team laid claim to the national championship and No. 1 status in the Associated Press poll when it finished undefeated, blanking Alabama 21–0 in its final game. Coach Jim Tatum walked away with Coach of the Year honors, and the team finished 10–1 after losing a close 7–0 contest to Oklahoma in the Orange Bowl.

Maryland's ACC rivalry
with the University of
Virginia spills over
into such competitions
as the Mock Trial
Program and the
Solar Decathlon.

The university's Mock Trial Team brandishes a
trophy it won in competition against dozens of other
universities nationwide.

Maryland teams have dominated no sport like they
have women's lacrosse. Since 1981, Terps women
have won five ACC championships and 10 national
championships. Between 1995 and 2001, Coach
Cindy Timchal's squad compiled a 140–5 record and
won seven consecutive NCAA championships.

A Walk through Maryland's Unfolding History

FROM ITS PRE-CIVIL WAR ROOTS as a tiny, private agricultural college and one of America's original land grant institutions, the University of Maryland has emerged as a public research university of national stature, highly regarded for its broad base of excellence in teaching and research as well as its commitment to diversity. Tragedy, triumph and the evidence of a rich history mark the progress of the university.

—1920—
A state-mandated consolidation of the renamed University of Maryland joins the institution located in College Park with that in Baltimore. Albert F. Woods, the president of Maryland State College, is named the first president of the University of Maryland. The graduate school awards its first doctorate degree, and Sigma Delta is the first sorority to be recognized on campus.

—1921—
The student newspaper is named the Diamondback in recognition of the Maryland terrapin.

—1921—
The College of Arts and Sciences is founded.

—1923—
The first May Day celebration begins a tradition that would continue for 38 years.

—1927—
A chapter of Omicron Delta Kappa, the national leadership society, is established on February 2, 1927. Women were not accepted into ODK until 1973.

—1932—
Ritchie Coliseum, the home of the university's men's basketball team, opens. Designed by Howard W. Cutler, the coliseum is named for Albert C. Ritchie, Maryland's governor from 1921 to 1935. That same year, Irene Knox, member of the women's rifle team, competes on the U.S. Olympic team.

—1934—
Mortar Board, the senior women's honorary society, is established.

—1935—
Harry Clifton "Curley" Byrd succeeds Pearson as president. A native of the state's Eastern Shore and a 1908 graduate of MAC, Byrd is a popular choice to succeed Pearson.

—1940—
Main Administration Building, with its distinctive copper roof, is completed.

Walk through Mary

Woods
the college
schools:
re, Engineering
hanic Arts,
Arts, Chemistry,
n, Home
ics and
te School.
rds the first
's degree to a
tudent, Grace B.

—1922—
Adele Stamp becomes the first dean of women at the university. The 103 female students enrolled for the fall term are more than four times the number enrolled two years before.

—1926—
Raymond A. Pearson, who served his country as Assistant Secretary of Agriculture during World War I, succeeds Albert F. Woods as president. Woods steps down but remains with the university's agriculture department for the next 22 years.

—1931—
The first doctorate degree is awarded to a woman, Daisy Inez Purdy. Her dissertation was titled "A Study of the Bacteriological Changes Produced During the Aging of Cured Hams."

—1933—
Members of the Class of 1933 donate the money for Testudo, the original campus statue of the diamondback terrapin that became the university's mascot. The 300-pound bronze statue is placed on a pedestal in front of Ritchie Coliseum and dedicated on Class Day in June.

—1938—
The School of Commerce, now the Robert H. Smith School of Business, is founded.

—1928—
The men's lacrosse team, founded in 1910, earns its first national title—a feat the team would repeat 11 more times.

—1944—
Congress passes the Servicemen's Readjustment Act of 1944. Better known as the GI Bill, it entitles veterans to federal subsidies for attending college.

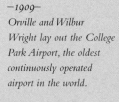

—1909—
Orville and Wilbur Wright lay out the College Park Airport, the oldest continuously operated airport in the world.

—1912—
A fire breaks out during a campus Thanksgiving dance. Before the blaze is contained, all dormitory rooms on campus as well as half of the classrooms and offices and most of the college's records are destroyed. The loss is estimated at $150,000, but no one is killed or injured. President Silvester is so distraught about the loss that he resigns his office.

—1917—
Regents name Albert F. Wood dean and acting president of the University of Minnesota, the first president of Maryland State College. Woods assumes leadership of large Reserve Officer Training Corps (ROTC) and Student Army Training Corps encampments.

—1888—
The Maryland General Assembly designates MAC as an Agricultural Experiment Station. The Hatch Act, passed by Congress in 1887, makes money available to agricultural colleges for that purpose.

—1890—
Congress passes the second Morrill Act. It provides for direct federal funding of technical education "without distinction of race or color."

—1894—
College of Engineering, now the A. James Clark School of Engineering, is founded.

—1914—
The Smith-Lever Act provides incentives to land grant colleges to create home economics courses and to establish the Cooperative Extension Service.

—1917—
Emma Jacobs receives M.S. degree.

A

—1891—
Pyon Su, the first Korean student to earn a degree at a U.S. college, is killed by a train shortly after graduating from MAC. He is buried in nearby Beltsville, Maryland.

—1892—
Richard W. Silvester, principal of Charlotte Hall Academy in St. Mary's County, Maryland, is named president of the college. During Silvester's 20 years in office, he lowers costs, erects seven buildings and emphasizes the college's agriculture and engineering offerings.

—1892—
The first football team loses all three of its games: St. John's, 50–0; Johns Hopkins, 62–0; and Episcopal High School, 16–0.

—1898—
President Silvester spends $24,000 to build Morrill Hall, the oldest academic building still in use during the university's 150th Anniversary year.

—1913—
Harry J. Patterson succeeds interim president Thomas H. Spence. Patterson is promoted to the presidency from his position as director of the Maryland Agricultural Experiment Station. Gamma Pi (now Sigma Nu) is the first fraternity officially recognized on campus.

—1915—
Students enrolled are the last required to wear a uniform. Among those is Chunjen Constant Chen, Shanghai, the first Chinese student, who will also earn a master's degree in 1920.

—1916—
After 60 years as a private and semi-public higher education facility, the Maryland Agricultural College becomes a full-fledged state institution. The renamed Maryland State College of Agriculture immediately admits female students.

—19
Pres
organ
into s
Agricu
and M
Liberal
Educat
Econom
Gradua
He awa
bachelo
female
Holmes

—1888—
The baseball team inaugurates intercollegiate athletics with games against St. John's College and the Naval Academy.

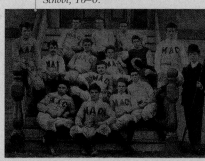

1856

—1858—
Landowner Charles Benedict Calvert sells 428 acres of his Riversdale Plantation for $20,000 for use as the new campus of the Maryland Agricultural College.

—1859—
The Maryland Agricultural College is dedicated on October 5. Four of the first 34 students are sons of Charles Benedict Calvert, who also serves as acting president following the one-month tenure of Benjamin Hallowell.

—1861—
Henry Onderdonk serves as president of the Maryland Agricultural College for much of the Civil War.

—1865—
Maryland Agricultural College is bankrupt, a victim of the Civil War. The college remains open as a preparatory school.

—1875—
William H. Parker, founder of the Confederate Naval Academy in Richmond, is named president of MAC. Like Jones, his predecessor, Parker emphasizes military training during his seven-year tenure.

—1873—
Samuel Jones, a West Point graduate and major general in the Confederate Army is named president of MAC. Taking office in one of the worst depressions of the 19th century, Jones inherits a debt-free college from the Reverend Samuel Regester.

—1883—
Augustine J. Smith, a Virginia businessman, succeeds Parker as president of Maryland Agricultural College. Smith embarks on a program of public relations, building bridges to the legislature, the state's farming community and members of the student body.

—1856—
The General Assembly charters the Maryland Agricultural College (MAC) on March 6. Trustees later issue stock to raise money for the college.

—1862—
On July 11, the first degrees are awarded by the Maryland Agricultural College to two students, William B. Sands (left) and Thomas Franklin.

—1869—
Methodist minister Samuel Regester succeeds Franklin Buchanan as president of MAC.

—1864—
The Maryland Legislature votes to accept a Morrill Land Grant from the U.S. Congress, which provides federal support for teaching agriculture, military tactics and mechanical arts. Meanwhile, the college grounds are the bivouac site for the Army of the Potomac's Ninth Army Corps and General Jubal T. Early's Confederate raiders during a three-month period in the spring and summer.

—1867—
George Washington Custis Lee, the son of Robert E. Lee and a former major general on Confederate President Jefferson Davis' staff, is appointed president of MAC. The ensuing uproar results in Lee resigning the position before he ever arrives on campus.

—1874—
Students are "required to wear a uniform when in attendance on divine services, inspections, parades, and drills, and on such other occasions as may be ordered."

—1874—
First graduate degrees awarded to the Rev. David Hall and F.A. Soper.

—1989—

The Board of Regents selects William E. Kirwan as president. A mathematician, Kirwan joins the faculty at Maryland in 1964 and during his 34-year career at the university, he is both a teacher and administrator, serving also as interim chancellor and provost.

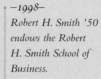

—1998—

Robert H. Smith '50 endows the Robert H. Smith School of Business.

—2001—

Faculty, students and administrators are aghast on a beautiful Tuesday morning in September when terrorists crash airplanes into the World Trade Center in Manhattan and the Pentagon in nearby Virginia. Just two weeks later, a tornado strikes campus, taking the lives of two students.

—2004—

The university breaks ground for a new biosciences building and M Square, a 124-acre research park.

—2005—

The Samuel Riggs IV Alumni Center opens, offering alumni an on-campus home.

—1994—

President Kirwan establishes the innovative College Park Scholars program.

—2002—

Coach Gary Williams, '68, guides the Terrapins to their first NCAA basketball championship on April 1, beating Indiana University, 64–52, in the final game.

—2005—

University Libraries acquires its 3 millionth volume. Previously, the Libraries reached the 1 million milestone in 1970 and 2 million in 1990.

—1996—

The University of Maryland breaks ground for what will become the Clarice Smith Performing Arts Center, named in honor of Washington artist and benefactor Clarice Smith.

—2002—

President C.D. Mote Jr. establishes a separate Foundation Board of Trustees, dedicated to the University of Maryland, College Park.

—2005—

Jeong H. Kim Engineering Research Building opens, defining the future of the Clark School of Engineering.

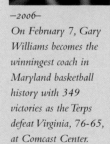

—1999—

Clayton Daniel Mote Jr. is inaugurated as the 27th leader of the University of Maryland. Mote, a professor of mechanical engineering, is recruited from the University of California–Berkeley, where he was a member of the faculty for 31 years and served as department chair and vice chancellor of university relations. Mote begins the tradition of Maryland Day, the university's open house, held on the last Saturday in April.

—2006—

On February 7, Gary Williams becomes the winningest coach in Maryland basketball history with 349 victories as the Terps defeat Virginia, 76-65, at Comcast Center.

—1990—

Daniel Podberesky files his suit on June 22, 1990, in the U.S. District Court for the District of Maryland to challenge the Banneker Scholarship Program. The U.S. Supreme Court denies the petition for writs of certiorari on May 22, 1995. The Banneker program is combined with the Francis Scott Key Scholarships for the 1995–96 academic year.

—2006—

The University of Maryland celebrates the 150th Anniversary of its chartering on March 6, 1856.

—2006—

—1967—
[S]chool of Architecture, [n]ow the School of Architecture, Planning, [a]nd Preservation, is [f]ounded.

[...] Kappa [...] a chapter [...]versity of

[1]966—
[Un]iversity Honors [pr]ogram established.

—1966—
First doctorate [is] awarded to an African American woman— Rebecca Carroll, [in] education.

[...]965—
[Th]e Tawes Fine Arts [Bu]ilding is erected. The [new] facility is named [for] J. Millard Tawes, [gov]ernor of Maryland [fro]m 1958 to 1966.

[...]
[S]chool of Library [In]formation [Studi]es, now the [Colleg]e of Information [Studie]s, is founded.

—1969—
The University of Maryland is granted membership into the Association of American Universities.

—1969—
Charles "Lefty" Driesell arrives at Maryland from tiny Davidson College in North Carolina to guide the Terrapins' basketball hopes in the rugged Atlantic Coast Conference.

—1972—
Congress passes and President Richard M. Nixon signs Title IX legislation that outlaws gender discrimination at any institution that receives federal appropriations.

—1970—
Wilson Elkins and the Board of Regents name Charles E. Bishop, who spent 24 years in agricultural economics and administration at universities in North Carolina, to the newly created chancellor position as head of the University of Maryland at College Park.

istory

—1974—
North Carolina State University defeats Maryland in the Atlantic Coast Conference championship game in what basketball fans consider one of the greatest ACC games ever played.

—1975—
Physicist Robert L. Gluckstern is named chancellor. During his seven-year tenure, Gluckstern upgrades the academic quality of the university by raising entrance standards. He also establishes scholarship programs including the Banneker minority scholarship.

—1981—
School of Public Affairs, now the School of Public Policy, is founded.

—1976—
In honor of the U.S. Bicentennial, the "M" Circle plantings are created by the Department of Physical Plant.

—1977—
The women's lacrosse team is organized. They will win 10 national championships, including seven straight from 1995 through 2001.

—1980—
The eight-year-old Undergraduate Library is named for R. Lee Hornbake, professor of industrial education, dean of the faculty and vice president for academic affairs.

—1982—
John B. Slaughter, the university's first African American chancellor, leads major advances in recruitment and retention of African American students and faculty during his six-year tenure.

—1985—
Enrollment at the University of Maryland at College Park hits an all-time high of 38,679 students.

—1986—
Len Bias, the Terrapins' All-American basketball player, dies of a drug overdose shortly after being selected as a top draft pick of the NBA's Boston Celtics. Bias' death casts a pall on the institution and becomes the impetus for review and improvement of standards in academic and athletic programs.

—1988—
The five University of Maryland institutions are reorganized with the six board-of-trustees-run institutions to create a university system. The University of Maryland is designated the flagship.

—1987—
The field hockey team wins the NCAA national championship, a feat they would repeat in 1993, 1999 and 2005.

—1986—
Four new colleges are founded, all previously part of other administrative entities: College of Life Sciences, College of Arts and Humanities, College of Computer, Mathematical and Physical Sciences, and College of Behavioral and Social Sciences.

—1957—
Queen Elizabeth II of Great Britain and her consort, Prince Philip, visit campus for a football game as the guests of President Elkins and Maryland Governor Theodore McKeldin. The contest is ever after known as "the Queen's Game."

—1964—
Phi Beta establishes at the Un Maryland

—1946—
Enrollment increases to nearly 10,000 students, many of them veterans attending school on the GI Bill.

—1947—
College of Journalism, which now bears the name of Philip Merrill, is founded.

—1953—
The Terrapins football squad finishes the 1953 season as the consensus national champions, and the school joins in the formation of the Atlantic Coast Conference.

—1955—
Student Union opens, which is later named to honor Adele H. Stamp, first dean of women.

—1955—
The Board of Regents officially recognizes the University Senate on September 23.

—1958—
The McKeldin Library, named for Maryland Governor Theodore McKeldin, opens for student use.

—1963—
Charles L. Fefferman, one of the nation's true mathematics geniuses, enrolls at the University of Maryland as a 14-year-old.

—
U
P.

land's Unfolding H

—1952—
The nondenominational Memorial Chapel is dedicated to honor members of the university community who lost their lives serving our country in the United States Armed Forces.

—1955—
The Terrapins defeat the University of Virginia, 67–55, in the first basketball game played at what would become Cole Field House the following year. The 14,500-seat gymnasium is named for Judge William P. Cole Jr., Class of 1910 and chairman of the Board of Regents from 1944 to 1956.

—1963—
Maryland is the first in the Atlantic Coast Conference to integrate four of its teams, beginning with Darryl Hill, football; swimming follows in 1964, men's basketball and track in 1965.

—1949—
College of Physical Education, Recreation and Health, now the College of Health and Human Performance, is founded.

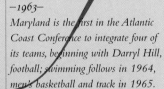

—1951—
Hiram Whittle, the first African American undergraduate student at the University of Maryland, enrolls. Three African American students also receive master's degrees in education.

—1954—
Wilson H. Elkins succeeds H.C. Byrd as the university's president. A football star at the University of Texas, Elkins goes on to become a Rhodes scholar and is president of Texas Western College when tapped for the Maryland job.

—1960—
Jim Henson, creator of the Muppets, graduates with a degree in home economics.

—
T
B
n.
fo
go
fro

—19
The
and
Serv
Col.
Stud

Enrollment Timeline

THE 34 STUDENTS ENROLLED IN 1859 when the first graduating class matriculated were for the most part white males from the local planter aristocracy. When the nation went to war in 1861, enrollment dropped to 25 students. It quadrupled by 1869 to 104 students, when the first class of post-Civil War students graduated.

Enrollment hovered around 200 students in the early years of the 20th century, and it wouldn't be until 1925 that enrollment at the University of Maryland topped 1,000 students. Enrollment quadrupled over the next 20 years to 4,176 students in 1945. Fueled by masses of returning veterans and funded by GI Bill benefits, enrollment doubled in 1946 to more than 8,500 students and climbed again in 1947 to 11,280 students.

Demographics played a major role in the next major enrollment jump. Enrollment gains averaged about 500 students a year between 1947 and 1963, although there were some years during that period when enrollment actually declined. Then the Baby Boomers started arriving at the university.

Enrollment jumped 3,000 students to 22,408 in 1964 and then added 10,000 students in the next four years to stand at 32,320 in 1968.

Enrollment reached its highest peak in 1985 with a student body of 38,679 that included 30,556 undergraduates. Shortly after legislation passed in 1988 designating the University of Maryland, College Park, as the flagship, focused efforts took hold to reduce the number of undergraduate students to improve the quality of the undergraduate experience for all. The buzzword was to make the "big store small." Enrollment in Fall 2005 was just over 35,300, including 25,442 undergraduates.

Furthermore, the makeup of the student body has changed dramatically since the first 34 students set foot at the Maryland Agricultural College. Today, women account for nearly half of the student body. To show how diverse the university has become, nearly one-third of the undergraduate students in 2005 are African American, Asian American, Hispanic or Native American.

Year	Enrollment
1859	34
1861	25
1869	104
1925	1,000
1945	4,176
1946	8,500
1947	11,280
1964	22,408
1968	32,320
1985	38,679
2005	35,300

CHAPTER 5

Programs of Distinction

‖ by Virginia W. Beauchamp

I'LL NEVER FORGET THE REACTION of one member of the committee appointed by Vice Chancellor George Callcott to explore whether the university should set up a program in Women's Studies. "Women's Studies!" that member said. "We might as well have Dog Studies!" This was back in 1972 when the content of any course you could think of outside of home economics was based on the experience of men. Every academic discipline was built on the unexpressed assumption that what was true for men also held true for women. Or, as our colleague seemed to affirm—that the experiences of half the human population did not matter.

This was a time of change and reflection—consciousness raising, it was called then—in the country at large. As a spin-off from the civil rights movement of the 1960s, women began to agitate for greater power. New organizations like NOW (National Organization for Women) and the National Women's Political Caucus were forming, and by 1972 Congress passed the Equal Rights Amendment. Voters of Maryland soon ratified it and adopted a state-level ERA.

Our committee recommended trying out an experimental program in Women's Studies, one of a handful of such academic programs in the United States. From that beginning in 1974, which I was privileged to lead, it has grown into a full-fledged department, one of 11 in the United States now offering the Ph.D. Under Professors Evelyn Beck and Claire Moses, two of its long-serving chairs, it became a leader, home of a major journal and headquarters of its national association.

Early in the 1970s, in and outside the classroom, female faculty, staff and women students were finding the university's general culture and governance both sexist and exclusionary. Led by Jean D. Grambs, one of about two dozen faculty women outside of home economics who were full professors, members of all these women's groups organized at least two general meetings to document their complaints.

Then-Chancellor Charles E. Bishop responded by creating an Advisory Commission on Women's Affairs that began holding hearings in January 1974. Women students described troubling experiences like sexual harassment in classroom settings and sexist content in assigned texts. Because of inadequate lighting, they were afraid to walk on campus at night.

The Diamondback riled up the university community by printing figures showing inequities in salaries of male and female faculty, and studies mandated by the passage of Title IX called attention to unequal resources in male and female athletic programs. On all these issues, university administrators took direct action and recruited women for upper-level faculty and staff positions. When hired in 1994, Deborah Yow was one of only 12 female athletics directors leading Division I athletic programs.

Finding the resources, overcoming the challenges and having the courage of one's convictions are the hallmarks of programs of distinction reflected throughout this institution. All began with a vision and the will to make it so. This is true for programs with long-standing reputation, such as physics, or newer endeavors not imagined only decades ago.

Maryland today is an institution that is nimble and adept. New academic programs like neural and cognitive sciences, as well as new centers like those in Persian studies and nanotechnology, are expanding and enriching our understanding of the world in which we live. We're a long way from the small agricultural college with which this all began!

A doctoral candidate in chemical engineering gains valuable research experience from a faculty mentor.

FROM THE TIME LT. JOHN D. FORD of the Engineer Corps of the U.S. Navy established a Department of Mechanical Engineering at Maryland in the waning days of the 19th century to the completion of the Jeong H. Kim Engineering Building in 2005, engineering has brought great renown to the university. The school took wing in 1944 when Glenn L. Martin, perhaps the pre-eminent aviation designer and manufacturer in pre–World War II North America, gave a generous endowment to the university that created the Glenn L. Martin College of Engineering and Aeronautical Sciences. Martin's gift laid the groundwork for the university's engineering initiatives today.

University researchers helped develop the system that delivered broadband Internet access to consumers via satellite.

University of Maryland benefactor Glenn L. Martin poses with a model of a World War II–era flying boat.

The Jeong H. Kim Engineering Building, opened in 2005, sets the stage for the next advances in engineering. Named for Clark School of Engineering alumnus, entrepreneur and philanthropist Jeong Kim, the building itself is a laboratory for 21st-century engineering technology.

The Space Systems Laboratory focuses its research on understanding and improving the ability to perform useful work in space. The lab has developed sophisticated robotics systems to assist astronauts in space, and its Neutral Buoyancy Facility is the only such test bed located at a university.

TODAY'S LIFE SCIENCES RESEARCHERS have moved far beyond the university's agricultural roots. The College of Chemical and Life Sciences includes some of the oldest departments at the university, as well as some of the newest. The departments of biology, entomology, chemistry and biochemistry, and cell biology and molecular genetics are joined by a number of research centers, including the Center for Biodiversity, the Joint Institute for Food Safety and Applied Nutrition, and the Laboratory for Biological Ultrastructure.

Earlene Armstrong, an associate professor of entomology at the university for nearly 30 years, has served as the primary advisor to hundreds of undergraduate students. In 2001, she garnered a Presidential Award for Excellence in Science, Mathematics and Engineering Mentoring.

Elizabeth Hook, the university's first female four-year graduate in 1920, was an entomology major.

An entomology lab at the dawn of the 20th century prepared Maryland's farmers to identify and deal with crop infestations.

An egg perched atop a double helix emphasizes the links between biosciences and traditional agricultural research.

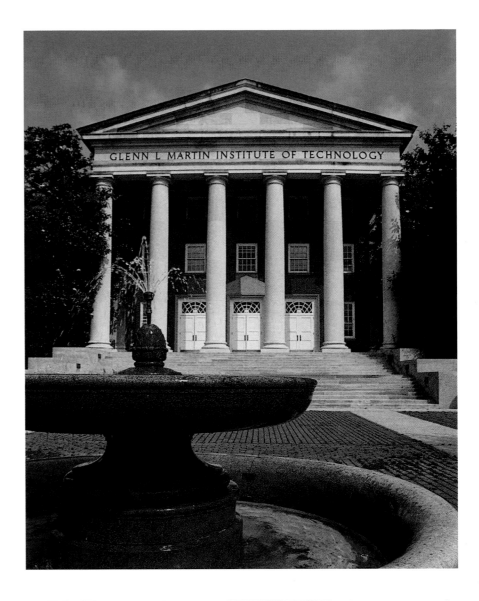

MATHEMATICS AND SCIENCE are at the fulcrum of the university's growing reputation as a world-class educational institution. Whether it is science faculty working in partnership with their counterparts at the National Institute of Standards and Technology or mathematics faculty strengthening math education in Baltimore City schools, faculty are both dedicated teachers and leaders in scholarship.

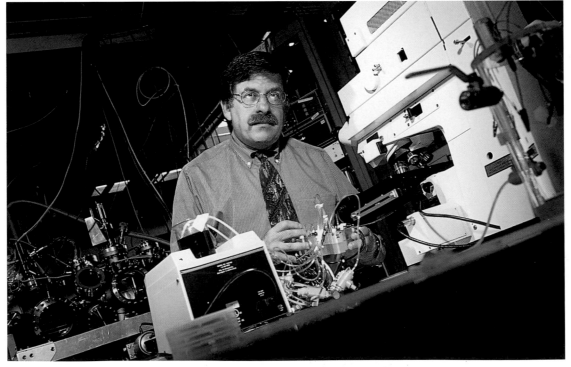

The university's Center for Integrated Nano Science and Engineering brings together cross-disciplinary teams of mathematicians, scientists and engineers for the adaptation of technologies such as oxide nanopowders to industrial applications.

The University of Maryland student experience encourages one-on-one interaction with faculty in their major field of study.

Sherry Scott-Joseph, Kimberly Weems and Tasha Inniss are awarded their doctorates in math in 2000, the first three African American women to earn Ph.D.'s in math at the university.

Students and faculty from the archaeology, anthropology and history departments gain a new appreciation for the past at the university's Caesarea Maritima excavation in Israel.

From world-renowned performers to student and community groups, the Clarice Smith Performing Arts Center provides a magnificent venue for creative expression.

ARTS AND HUMANITIES AT THE UNIVERSITY OF MARYLAND run the gamut from the study of languages and culture to the performing arts to international studies programs. The Clarice Smith Performing Arts Center integrates music, dance, theatre and a high-tech library in a "village" of the performing arts. The School of Languages, Literatures and Cultures, in cooperation with the Center for the Advanced Study of Language, the Persian Studies Institute, the Confucius Institute, the National Foreign Language Center and the UM Institute for Advanced Computer Studies have made the university a national leader in the study of languages and linguistics.

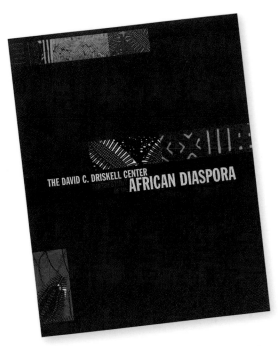

The David C. Driskell Center for the Study of the African Diaspora seeks to preserve the rich heritage of African American visual art and culture while encouraging future artists of color to develop their talents and skills.

David Poeppel, a member of the linguistics faculty, explores the connection between the brain and linguistics ability.

Noted pianist André Watts, an artist-in-residence at Maryland for three years, instructs a doctoral candidate in piano performance.

TEAMWORK AND STUDENT ACHIEVEMENT have been
hallmarks of the learning experience at Maryland in recent years. Students
learn how to interact with their peers in setting goals and working
through complicated problems toward a common solution, typified by the
Hinman Campus Entrepreneurship Opportunities (CEOs) Program. First
and second year students can avail themselves of the College Park Scholars
Program, a community of a dozen special living-learning programs. Other
students participate in Gemstone, a unique program with roots in the
university's engineering school that integrates technology and social issues
into team research projects guided by a faculty mentor and spanning all
four years of the undergraduate experience.

*A Hinman mentor reviews
a business plan for two
undergraduates.*

*Anne Arundel Hall includes
the offices of the university's
highly selective Honors
living/learning program and
serves as a residence hall for
some of the students. Each
year, approximately 700
students are invited into the
Honors program.*

In the early 1990s, mechanical engineering students designed, built and raced the "Pride of Maryland," a solar-powered car that competed in a series of races held in the United States, Australia and Japan. The non-polluting vehicle is shown here taking a ride down Pennsylvania Ave. in our nation's capital.

College Park Scholars participate in classes that take them beyond the borders of the campus.

Members of the University of Maryland team participating in the Solar Decathlon discuss refinements they intend to incorporate into their energy-efficient home.

The Anwar Sadat Chair for Peace and Development continues to be a force for peaceful resolution of the conflicts in the Middle East.

The Robert H. Smith School of Business makes its home in the functionally elegant Van Munching Hall, opened in 1993 and expanded in 2002. From this vantage point, the school delivers academic, professional and social experiences necessary to help prepare students to lead 21st-century organizations.

The Department of Astronomy, which has made international headlines for its leadership role in NASA's Deep Impact mission, is located in the Computer Space Sciences Building, shown at right.

WITH ITS PROXIMITY TO THE WASHINGTON-BALTIMORE CORRIDOR, it's no surprise that the university is renowned for its public policy and social sciences focus. Faculty members are called upon on an almost daily basis by the national and international media to comment on the latest public policy issue.

The College of Education's Center for Young Children is a full-day educational program that serves as a demonstration school for training students and as an observation and research facility for early childhood development.

For the past decade, the Brody Forum in the School of Public Policy has brought renowned leaders and public policy experts to the University of Maryland to increase discussion and awareness of topics of national and international importance.

IN MANY WAYS, PHYSICS IS THE KEY to unlocking the secrets of the universe, and Maryland's physics department has been in the forefront of the discipline for more than a century. Early experiments in gases and lighting led to practical applications in the state's homes and farms. In the 1950s and 1960s, because of its proximity to NASA facilities in the Baltimore-Washington corridor, the department became heavily involved in the study of rocketry. Under the tutelage of John S. Toll, physics at the university grew to become one of the largest such departments in the nation, with more than 30 different fields of physics under study.

A 1950s-era research rocket stands ready for carrying Maryland's name into space.

John S. Toll was both physicist and administrator. During his long career, Toll served as chair of the physics department and later president of the university system.

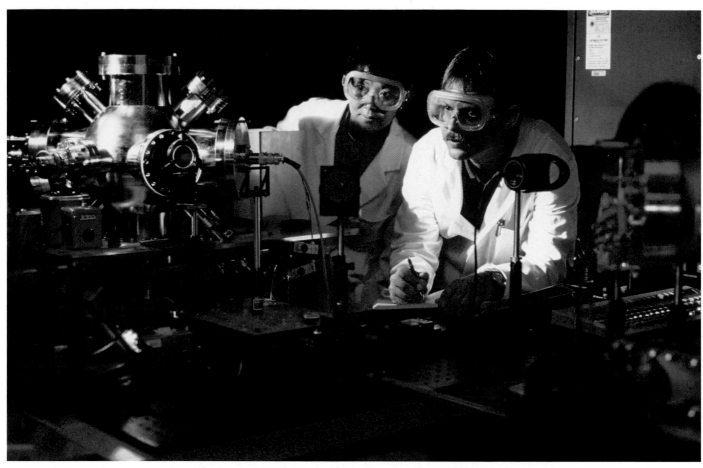

Superconductivity is a 21st-century research focus of the physics department.

The physics lab in 1891 was concerned with experiments designed to improve the lives of the state's farmers.

– CHAPTER 6 –
Enduring Landmarks & Touchstones

III *by David C. Driskell* CERTAINLY A QUALITY ACADEMIC PROGRAM is a must in the equation of greatness but so are the significant touchstones and landmarks that give the place an important visual and historical presence. Significantly observable is the manner in which the university has come to address the social issues that once limited its outlook on the omissions of history that center on race, gender and diversity of programs.

As a result of this enlightened review of the university's often overlooked history, it has garnered to itself a unique and enduring legacy that now serves as a model among the great universities of our nation. And, out of that good fortune, several important programs are evident in the arts, humanities and social sciences that help move the

university to address the impending relevance of a more colorless humanity.

Visibly evident is the Nyumburu Cultural Center, which promotes the scholarly exchange and artistic engagement of African Diaspora culture, as do the activities of the center that bears my name and whose mission is to preserve the rich

heritage of African American visual art and culture.

Equally important to the uniqueness of this historic institution is how well-known university landmarks and touchstones blend favorably with those of recent years. Consider the elegant lines seen in Memorial Chapel, now a campus landmark beyond a half-century old, with recently built structures such as the Samuel Riggs IV Alumni Center and the functional elegance of Comcast Center, to name only a few.

Indeed, these well-known campus landmarks, including the "M" Circle, where flowers accentuate the beauty of our entry to the main campus, resonate iconically in the minds of those who visit this historic

place. The winding roads that encircle the campus, a city within a city, bring us past beautiful buildings that house the great disciplines of learning that have fed the minds of a learned class of distinguished alumni over a period of 150 years.

These roads remind us of the places we have gone beyond the campus as well as the historical events that have taken place here. Yet we are reminded in our remembrances that we continue, as these winding roads change and go in new directions, on our spiraling journey to human greatness.

Think of how interesting, how different, how refined and how significantly mature our pursuit down the paths of learning shall have taken us another 150 years from

now. Our landmarks will have increased in numbers. Our touchstones will be ever more endearing. There will be new places of learning and new technologies that are all but unfathomable to the human mind. Remaining intact will be our inheritance of the classical ways of learning from an ancient past.

It is my sincere hope that the University of Maryland will continue to be a leader among the great universities of the world in the years ahead—having had an anchor deeply cast in the promotion of knowledge and truth in the beginning decade of the 21st century.

FOR GENERATIONS OF STUDENTS, faculty
and alumni, Maryland's campus conjures up
memories of McKeldin Mall, Testudo, Rossborough
Inn, Memorial Chapel and the Henson statue. All
are uniquely Maryland, and all mean different
things to different generations. Campus landmarks
and touchstones live on long after one generation of
students gives way to another.

*From the air, the campus is a sea of emerald, dotted
with a built environment embracing a century-and-a-
half of architectural styles.*

Fall brings out a collage of color and light that bathes the campus in hues of red and gold.

The rising sun casts a growing light on the sundial that anchors the center of McKeldin Mall. The astronomical timepiece was a gift of the Class of 1965, the Department of Physics and Astronomy, and the friends of Professor Uco Van Wijk, who died in 1966. The Class of 1990 donated money to renovate the campus landmark.

The Campus Recreation Center is one of the university's newer landmarks. Opened in early 1998, the $40 million center includes a world-class natatorium and adjacent outdoor pool that have been the site of numerous championship swimming events, including the ACC championships, the FINA World Cup and YMCA national meets.

◀ The cupola atop H.J. Patterson Hall casts a beacon against a nighttime sky. Built in 1935, this building originally housed the School of Arts and Sciences.

PERHAPS THE LANDMARK that most immediately identifies the University of Maryland in the minds of students, faculty and alumni is Testudo. Donated by the Class of 1933, sculptor Aristide Cianfarani cast the terrapin in bronze, and Testudo found his first resting space on a pedestal in front of Ritchie Coliseum. In the early years, students from rival schools—most often Johns Hopkins and Navy—frequently kidnapped Testudo for ransom. In the 1950s, the statue was reinforced with steel rods and cement and placed in front of Byrd Stadium. The 1,000-pound statue made its most recent voyage in 1965, when it came to rest on a pedestal in front of McKeldin Library.

The big M signifying Maryland is evident to the discerning eye just about anywhere one might look on campus, including in the pedestal beneath the Testudo statue, engraved in stone on a cornice, inlaid in brick or enclosing the Moxley Gardens of the Riggs Alumni Center.

WHEN THE MEMORIAL CHAPEL WAS BUILT IN 1952, Maryland students and alumni were fighting and dying on the frozen hills of Korea. Nearly 200 students and alumni had lost their lives in the service of their country during two World Wars, and it was to honor those who had made the supreme sacrifice that the chapel was built. No state funds were used to build the nondenominational chapel and equip it with a carillon and a pipe organ.

The University of Maryland Chorus performs Joseph Haydn's oratorio, "The Creation," at Memorial Chapel to conclude its 30th season in 1998, under the direction of Paul Traver, who retired that year. Below, the "topping off" of the spire is captured here in this 1951 photo.

On Sept. 12, 2001, the Omicron Delta Kappa (ODK) fountain was ringed with flowers as the university community gathered for a memorial service to pay tribute to those who died in the Sept. 11 terrorist attacks in New York and Washington, D.C.

The ODK fountain at the center of McKeldin Mall was donated by this leadership society and its alumni in 1990.

One of the best views of the nine-acre expanse of McKeldin Mall is from the portico of Jiménez, Hall. Built in 1962, the hall honors Spanish poet Juan Ramón Jiménez, who taught Spanish in the 1940s and early 1950s before winning the Nobel Prize in Literature in 1956.

The snow-covered ground casts a cold light on
H.J. Patterson Hall and the stone monoliths of the
"Night-Day" sculpture framing the building.

The bronze statue of Kermit
the Frog and his creator,
alumnus Jim Henson, share
a bench at the entrance to the
Stamp Student Union. One
of the newest landmarks,
it is also one of the most
popular spots for photo
opportunities.

The wrought iron 1910
ornamental arch was a gift of
the Class of 1910 and was
erected in 1941.

The new Samuel Riggs IV
Alumni Center, designed
by award-winning architect
and alumnus Hugh Newell
Jacobsen '51, '93 (Honorary
Doctorate), opened its doors
in Spring 2005. In close
proximity to both Byrd
Stadium and the Clarice
Smith Performing Arts
Center, the new home for
alumni boasts interior spaces
both grand and intimate.
Outside, the beautifully
planted Moxley Gardens
(pictured at right) provide a
tranquil retreat.

McKeldin Library at night beckons scholars eager to discover the treasures that lie within.

The worthy successor to Ritchie Coliseum and Cole Field House, the Comcast Center, home of the Terrapins' basketball program since 2002, will likely become one of the university's 21st-century athletic landmarks.

CHAPTER 7

The Terrapin Spirit

‖ *by Brenda Brown Rever*

FORTY YEARS! When I look at the differences that abound today at Maryland it seems like a century could have passed since I graduated. Those of us who were students in the early and mid-'60s remember a typical—for that time—scene. Homecoming parades, yellow mums to wear and funny purple drinks passed out at football games that caused card sections to run amuck. We saw Ella Fitzgerald, Dustin Hoffman, Bob Hope, the Kingston Trio, Harry Belafonte—and Peter, Paul and Mary were there, too.

College was fun for me, but I took for granted that I would attend the University of Maryland. I did not take advantage of all that was offered academically, and I took for granted that there were different rules for "boys and girls." We didn't call ourselves men and women then. We accepted that girls had curfews and boys didn't. We accepted that we could only wear "slacks" to school on days that were below 32 degrees.

Our spirit was directed at football games and social events. I recall being able to attend any basketball game at Cole Field

House and sitting at mid-court. There may have been a couple hundred other people watching a game. So you may ask yourself: "Why is she writing an essay on spirit?" The answer is: I love the University of Maryland—now more than ever. It took me about 25 years after I graduated to catch the spirit, but catch it I did.

The university had lost me but I found it. I called the alumni office one day and said, "I am reading about all kinds of great programs that you now offer and courses that we never had a chance to choose. Could I bring about 50 women out to experience what Maryland has to offer today?" We came, we saw, we participated and we were impressed with our school. That convinced me to become involved.

Eventually, becoming a member of the university's Board of Visitors and then the foundation's Board of Trustees enabled me to experience afresh the camaraderie of the University of Maryland family today. I also met my husband Philip Rever on the board. Talk about catching the spirit!

I think that through my "returned" experiences with the university, I learned what was needed to make a university great today. We needed to be able to compete nationwide for top students and faculty, and to contribute to the state's economy and development. We needed to keep growing academically, professionally, fiscally—and "spirit"-ually.

And, so we have. Today, Maryland is as hard to get in academically as it is to snag

a ticket to a basketball game. The spirit and enthusiasm is so great that you better finish any conversations before you come into our new Comcast Center. For the first time in years, Byrd Stadium is full for home football games. The women's lacrosse team set records by winning the national championship seven years in a row—a feat that earned a trip to the White House.

If you haven't been to the Clarice Smith Performing Arts Center, make a reservation for a performance today. The theaters are magnificent and the performances outstanding. Nearby, the new Samuel Riggs IV Alumni Center gives alumni a place to truly call our own. Did I say we had come a long way in 40 years? See for yourself. You too will catch the spirit!

EACH YEAR, *PRINCETON REVIEW* RANKS more
than 300 colleges and universities nationwide to determine
the best schools in a number of categories. According to
the 2005 publication, Maryland is the school that is
most supportive of its college athletic teams.
That should come as no surprise to
anyone who has witnessed the
Fear the Turtle spirit
of recent years.

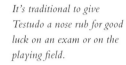

Gimme an M …
Gimme an A …
Gimme an R …

It's traditional to give Testudo a nose rub for good luck on an exam or on the playing field.

Maryland Day, instituted by President Mote in 1999 during his inaugural year and held the last Saturday in April ever since, now attracts as many as 70,000 people to the university.

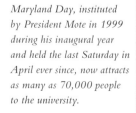

THE ARE FEW EVENTS in contemporary sports that can compare to Atlantic Coast Conference football or basketball games. Maryland has been a member of the ACC for more than a half-century, and the prospect of a showdown with North Carolina at Byrd or a late-season conference game with Duke at the Comcast Center is enough to send Terrapin fans into orbit.

Maryland fans show their disdain for opposing teams by reading and rattling newspapers while the other team is announced, as this Maryland crowd at Cole is doing in 1995.

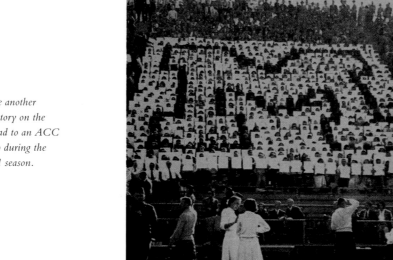

Fans celebrate another Maryland victory on the Terrapins' road to an ACC championship during the magical 2001 season.

Maryland fans have always proudly displayed the "M," as this card section shows in this vintage 1950 photo.

The Lyle gun in the end zone records another Maryland score during a late-season game sometime in the 1970s. It's a Terp tradition that dates back to 1960.

A fan flaunted his red-and-white allegiance to the Terps whenever he drove this Volkswagen Beetle to games during the 1986 season.

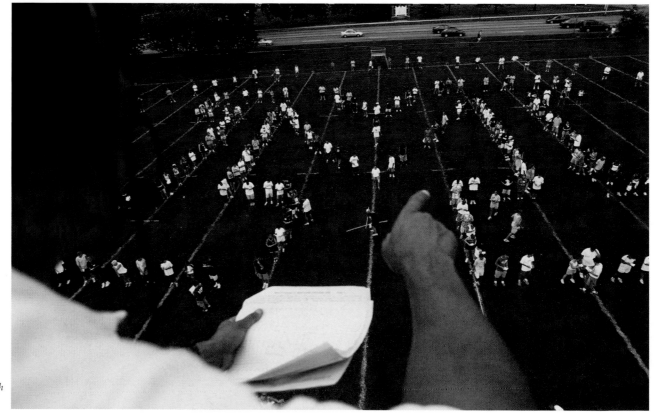

Director L. Richmond Sparks leads the Mighty Sound of Maryland through its pregame routine.

THE PAGEANTRY OF BIG-TIME COLLEGE FOOTBALL
wouldn't be nearly the spectacle it is without the participation of
the Maryland Marching Band. Maryland's student band has been
enriching the experience for generations of fans since its founding
as a cadet band by L.G. Smith, the Maryland Agricultural College
bugler. Today, the Mighty Sound of Maryland is more than 270
students strong.

*The 30-plus-member cadet band poses on the steps
of Calvert Hall at what was then Maryland State
College of Agriculture in 1917.*

*The Mighty Sound of
Maryland performs at every
home game and one away
game each year. Marching
Band is offered as a 2-credit
course each fall semester.*

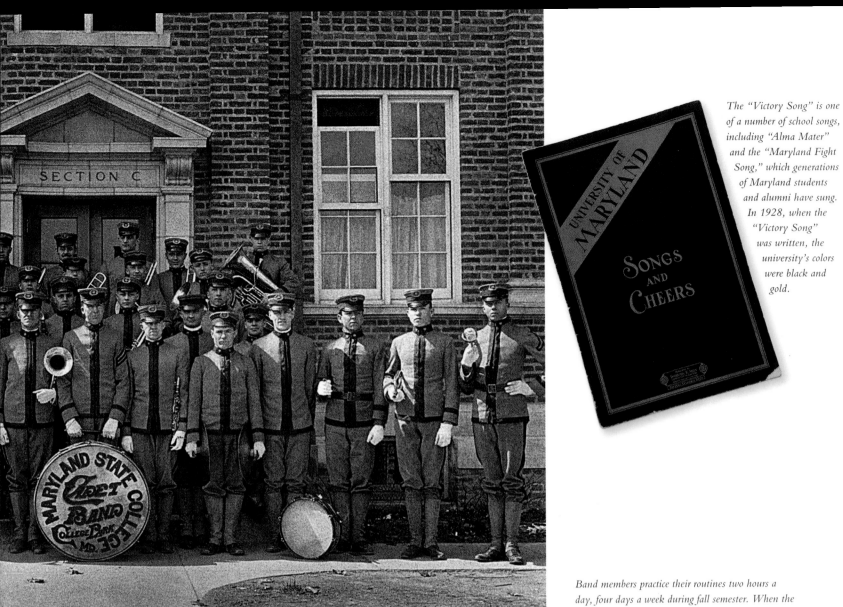

The "Victory Song" is one of a number of school songs, including "Alma Mater" and the "Maryland Fight Song," which generations of Maryland students and alumni have sung. In 1928, when the "Victory Song" was written, the university's colors were black and gold.

Band members practice their routines two hours a day, four days a week during fall semester. When the Terrapins are victorious at Byrd, the Mighty Sound of Maryland marches back to the Clarice Smith Performing Arts Center with their hats perched backwards on their heads.

The Testudo mascot expresses Maryland's number-one ranking in the hearts of its fans.

A homecoming float in the 1950s incorporated the turtle theme into the wire and papier-mâché structure.

SINCE "CURLEY" BYRD FIRST INTRODUCED the idea of designating the Maryland diamondback terrapin as the school's mascot in the early 1930s, the turtle has defined Maryland athletics. Up until that time, Maryland's teams had been known as Aggies—for the predecessor Maryland Agricultural College—or Old Liners, for Maryland's nickname, the Old Line State.

In the days before Testudo bulked up to his present 1,000-plus pounds weight, the turtle was frequently the victim of kidnapping plots by rival schools. These three Johns Hopkins students were captured trying to spirit the 300-pound Testudo to their dormitory in Baltimore in 1947 and were shorn of their locks by Maryland students as punishment for their misdeeds.

Sigma Phi Epsilon sponsored this candy box float in the homecoming parade in November 1950. Maryland beat George Washington 23–7 before a crowd of nearly 19,000 fans.

Leave it to the engineering students to design a giant, mechanical Attack Testudo in the late 1960s to strike fear into the hearts of Terrapin foes everywhere.

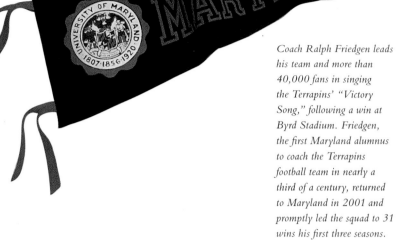

Coach Ralph Friedgen leads his team and more than 40,000 fans in singing the Terrapins' "Victory Song," following a win at Byrd Stadium. Friedgen, the first Maryland alumnus to coach the Terrapins football team in nearly a third of a century, returned to Maryland in 2001 and promptly led the squad to 31 wins his first three seasons.

TERRAPIN SPIRIT is manifested in dozens of ways, but none so all encompassing as a football Saturday at Byrd. Cheers, pennants, singing and chants all play out against a sea of red, dazzling the senses.

Passengers deplaning at the Southwest Airlines gates at the Baltimore/Washington International Thurgood Marshall Airport are greeted by the Fear the Turtle campaign touting the University of Maryland as a formidable academic and economic force.

Cheerleaders have been performing the Locomotive and Yea, Maryland cheers since 1917. Females first joined the all-male cheerleading squad in 1925, and in 2003, the university added women's cheerleading as a competitive sport, the first such varsity program in the United States.

Contemporary Terrapin fans have grown accustomed to seeing Fear the Turtle messages around the state, as on this billboard along the I-95 approach to Baltimore.

The Maryland band whips fans into a red-and-white frenzy.

CHAPTER 8

150 Notable Alumni

||| IN A HISTORY THAT SPANS 150 YEARS, the University of Maryland has had countless alumni who have made contributions to society. This Anniversary gives us the opportunity to showcase 150 alumni who have distinguished themselves in a breadth of fields or had a significant impact on the university through their involvement. They represent only a small portion of the notable alumni of the University of Maryland.

Harry C. "Curley" Byrd

CARMEN BALTHROP, 1971, B.M., MUSIC/VOICE
Internationally acclaimed soprano who has performed at the White House, the Metropolitan Opera and around the world; voice professor at Maryland; Alumni Hall of Fame member.

ZVI BARZILAY, 1973, B.S., ARCHITECTURE
President and COO of Toll Brothers, a builder of luxury homes; has served as professor of architecture and urban design.

ROBERT D. BASHAM, 1970, B.S., BUSINESS ADMINISTRATION
Co-founder of Outback Steakhouse, the company that brought the "bloomin' onion" to America.

RAJAT BASU, 1977, PH.D., PHYSICS
Honored as a "Hero of Chemistry" for his contribution to the solution of global ozone depletion.

GAIL BERMAN, 1978, B.A., THEATRE
Producer of live theater, television (including *American Idol* and *24*) and film; president of Paramount Pictures.

CARL BERNSTEIN, 1961–64
Investigative journalist best known for his Pulitzer Prize–winning Watergate reporting for *The Washington Post*.

ERIC BILLINGS, 1977, B.S., ECONOMICS AND FINANCE
Chairman and CEO of Friedman Billings Ramsey Group, a top 10 investment bank.

ADISAI BODHARAMIK, 1971, PH.D., ELECTRICAL ENGINEERING
Thailand's Education Minister and former Minister of Commerce; a telecommunications pioneer in Thailand; Alumni Hall of Fame member.

ROBERT C. BONNER, 1963, B.A., GOVERNMENT AND POLITICS
Former commissioner of the U.S. Customs and Border Protection service; former director of the U.S. Drug Enforcement Agency.

TIM BRANT, 1973, B.S., JOURNALISM
National and metro-Washington area sportscaster; has covered the Olympics as well as professional and college sports.

SERGEY BRIN, 1993, B.S., MATHEMATICS AND COMPUTER SCIENCE
Turned a graduate school project into Google, the world's largest and most popular search engine.

KENNETH D. BRODY, 1964, B.S., ELECTRICAL ENGINEERING
Former chairman and president of the U.S. Export-Import Bank; had a long career with Goldman Sachs.

JOHN BROPHY, 1971, B.A., HISTORY
Executive vice president of ACS; a pioneer in outsourcing solutions for government agencies; UMCP Foundation Board of Trustees.

LESTER BROWN, 1959, M.S., AGRICULTURAL ECONOMICS; 1976, HONORARY DOCTORATE
Founder of World Watch Institute, one of the first environmental advocacy groups.

VICKY BULLETT, 1990, B.G.S., GENERAL STUDIES
Former WNBA star with the Charlotte Sting and Washington Mystics; U.S. Olympic gold medalist in 1988 and bronze medalist in 1992.

WALDO BURNSIDE, 1949, B.S., PERSONNEL ADMINISTRATION
Retired president of the retail giant that included "Woodies" department stores; helped create the Regents and Banneker/Key Scholarship programs at the university; UMCP Foundation Board of Trustees; Alumni Hall of Fame member.

HARRY C. "CURLEY" BYRD,
1908, B.S., ENGINEERING
Legendary football coach and
president; guided the university
through the Great Depression and
World War II; Alumni Hall of Fame
member.

DENNIS CARDOZA, 1982, B.A.,
GOVERNMENT AND POLITICS
U.S. Representative for the 18th
District of California; first in his
family to graduate from college.

AL CAREY, 1974, B.A., URBAN
STUDIES
President of PepsiCo Sales; has been
involved in the food and beverage
industry for his entire career; UMCP
Foundation Board of Trustees.

JERRY CEPPOS, 1969, B.S.,
JOURNALISM
Former vice president for news with
Knight-Ridder; former executive
editor of *The San Jose Mercury News*.

ROBERT CHANDLER, 1934,
PH.D., HORTICULTURE; 1975,
HONORARY DOCTORATE
Devoted to increasing food
production for the world's hungry;
awarded the World Food Prize in
1988; Alumni Hall of Fame member.

SOO YOUNG CHANG, 1968, M.S.,
ELECTRICAL ENGINEERING;
1971, PH.D., ELECTRICAL
ENGINEERING
Former president of Pohang
University of Science and Technology
in South Korea.

CONNIE CHUNG, 1969, B.S.,
JOURNALISM
News reporter and anchor for all three
major television networks; recipient of
three Emmys and a Peabody Award;
Alumni Hall of Fame member.

MARK CIARDI, 1983, B.S.,
MARKETING
Producer of films including *The
Rookie* and *Miracle*; played professional
baseball for one year.

Parren Mitchell

A. JAMES CLARK, 1950, B.S.,
CIVIL ENGINEERING
Benefactor of the A. James Clark
School of Engineering; construction
entrepreneur whose company built
more than 20 university buildings as
well as Camden Yards and Lincoln
Center; UMCP Foundation Board
of Trustees; Alumni Hall of Fame
member.

WILLIAM P. COLE JR., 1910, B.S.,
CIVIL ENGINEERING
Served on the Board of Regents for
a quarter-century; namesake of the
Cole Student Activities Building;
Alumni Hall of Fame member.

MARY STALLINGS COLEMAN,
1935, B.A., ENGLISH; 1978,
HONORARY DOCTORATE
Named the first female Chief Justice
of the Michigan Supreme Court in
1979; Alumni Hall of Fame member.

BOB CORLISS, 1976, B.A.,
GOVERNMENT AND POLITICS
President and CEO of The Athlete's
Foot, a leader in athletic footwear
stores; a torch bearer for the Salt Lake
City Olympics in 2002.

MICHAEL DANA, 1981, B.S.,
MARKETING
A real estate investment banking
professional; head of Onex Real
Estate Partners; UMCP Foundation
Board of Trustees.

Connie Chung

GEORGE DANTZIG, 1936,
B.A., MATHEMATICS; 1976,
HONORARY DEGREE
National Academy of Sciences
member; laid the foundation for much
of the field of systems engineering
through the invention of linear
programming.

LARRY DAVID, 1970, B.A.,
HISTORY
Comedic actor and writer; co-creator
of the Emmy Award–winning *Seinfeld*;
writer and star of HBO's *Curb Your
Enthusiasm*; Alumni Hall of Fame
member.

RAYMOND DAVIS, 1937, B.S.,
CHEMISTRY/INDUSTRIAL; 1940,
M.S., CHEMISTRY/INDUSTRIAL
2002 Nobel Laureate in physics for
his contributions to astrophysics,
particularly for the detection of
cosmic neutrinos; Alumni Hall of
Fame member.

RUTH DAVIS, 1952, M.A.,
MATHEMATICS; 1955, PH.D.,
MATHEMATICS
Computer science pioneer; helped
design some early computers and
satellite projects; one of the first
female math Ph.D. recipients; UMCP
Foundation Board of Trustees; Alumni
Hall of Fame member.

DOMINIQUE DAWES, 2002, B.A.,
SPEECH
Three-time U.S. Olympic gymnast
who garnered bronze and gold
medals; involved with organizations
inspiring girls to achieve their full
potential.

CEDRIC DENT, 1997, PH.D.,
MUSIC
Baritone vocalist, arranger and
producer with the group Take 6;
seven-time Grammy Award winner.

MICHAEL DINGMAN,
1951–53, 1989, HONORARY
DOCTORATE
President of the Shipston Group;
benefactor of the university's
entrepreneurship center.

EDWARD DOWNEY, 1952, B.S.,
ADMINISTRATION/LOGISTICS
Chairman of Empower IT and
Downey Communications, publisher
of magazines for military families;
native of College Park who delivered
newspapers to Curley Byrd's home;
UMCP Foundation Board of Trustees.

MILO DOWNEY, 1927, B.S.,
AGRICULTURE; 1940, M.A.
AGRICULTURE EDUCATION
Pioneer of national 4-H education
program expansion and agriculture
extension programs.

Mary Stallings Coleman

Jim Henson with Muppets

LEONARD J. ELMORE, 1978, B.A., ENGLISH
Great Terrapin basketball player; had a 10-year career in the NBA; first NBA veteran to earn a law degree from Harvard; UMCP Foundation Board of Trustees; Alumni Hall of Fame member.

GORDON ENGLAND, 1961, B.S., ELECTRICAL ENGINEERING
Deputy Secretary of Defense; first deputy secretary in the U.S. Department of Homeland Security; former Secretary of the Navy; former executive with General Dynamics.

GEARY FRANCIS "SWEDE" EPPLEY, 1920, B.S., AGRICULTURE; 1926, M.S., AGRICULTURE
Had a 50-year academic and administrative career at the university; first president of the Atlantic Coast Conference; Alumni Hall of Fame member.

NORMAN "BOOMER" ESIASON, 1984, B.G.S., GENERAL STUDIES
All-America quarterback at Maryland; 14-year NFL career included Cincinnati's appearance in Super Bowl XXIII; NFL Most Valuable Player in 1988; national figure in the fight against cystic fibrosis; sports broadcaster; Alumni Hall of Fame member.

JOHN "JACK" FABER, 1926, B.S., BACTERIOLOGY; 1927, M.S., BACTERIOLOGY; 1937, PH.D., BACTERIOLOGY
Longtime chair of the Department of Microbiology; also coached the lacrosse team, which won nine national championships; Alumni Hall of Fame member.

ROBERT FACCHINA, 1977, B.S., FOOD SCIENCE
President and CEO of Johanna Foods, yogurt and juice drink manufacturer; provided fleet of 18-wheelers displaying Fear the Turtle and 150th Anniversary messages; sponsor of cutting-edge cancer treatment; UMCP Foundation Board of Trustees.

CHARLES FEFFERMAN, 1966, B.S., MATHEMATICS; 1979, HONORARY DOCTORATE
Youngest recipient of the prestigious Fields Medal in mathematics; graduated from the university at age 17, received Ph.D. at age 20; professor at Princeton since 1973; Alumni Hall of Fame member.

RAUL FERNANDEZ, 1990, B.A., ECONOMICS
Chairman, president and CEO of Object Video; founder of Proxicom; part owner of the Washington Capitals hockey team.

ROSARIO FERRÉ, 1987, PH.D., SPANISH
Considered Puerto Rico's leading woman of letters; her novel, *The House on the Lagoon*, was a finalist for the National Book Award in 1995.

CARLETON "CARLY" FIORINA, 1980, M.B.A.
Former president and CEO of Hewlett-Packard; former president of Lucent Technologies; in 2004, was appointed by the White House to the U.S. Space Commission; Alumni Hall of Fame member.

ROBERT E. FISCHELL, 1953, M.S., PHYSICS; 1996, HONORARY DOCTORATE
Inventor with more than 200 patents; responsible for medical devices including the stent, rechargeable pacemaker and implantable insulin pump; benefactor of biomedical engineering at the university; UMCP Foundation Board of Trustees; Alumni Hall of Fame member.

JON D. FRANKLIN, 1970, B.S., JOURNALISM
Recipient of the Pulitzer Prize for feature writing in 1979 and for explanatory journalism in 1985; returned to his alma mater as Philip Merrill Professor of Journalism; Alumni Hall of Fame member.

RALPH FRIEDGEN, 1970, B.S., PHYSICAL EDUCATION; 1972, M.A., PHYSICAL EDUCATION
Head football coach at Maryland; named the consensus national Coach of the Year in 2001 after leading Maryland to its first ACC championship since 1985.

FRED FUNK, 1980, B.S., LAW ENFORCEMENT
Professional golfer; turned pro in 1981 but coached golf at the university from 1982–88; in 2005, achieved distinction as the oldest player to win the Players Championship.

THOMAS C. GALLAGHER, 1970, B.S., MARKETING
President, chairman and CEO of Genuine Parts Co.; rang the opening bell at the New York Stock Exchange in 2003.

ALMA GILDENHORN, 1953, B.A., EDUCATION/SOCIAL STUDIES
Washington civic leader and philanthropist; former co-chair and trustee of the Kennedy Center; holds leadership roles with the Aspen Institute, Friends of Art and Preservation in Embassies and Swiss American Cultural Exchange Council; UMCP Foundation Board of Trustees.

JOSEPH B. GILDENHORN, 1951, B.S., BUSINESS AND PUBLIC ADMINISTRATION
Founding partner in The JBG Companies; former U.S. Ambassador to Switzerland; chair of the Woodrow Wilson International Center for Scholars; UMCP Foundation Board of Trustees.

DAVID GOLDFARB, 1979, B.S., ACCOUNTING
Chief administrative officer and executive vice president of Lehman Brothers Holdings; has extensive experience in the financial services industry.

BARRY GOSSETT, 1958–60
CEO of Acton Mobile Industries; benefactor of athletics and academics at the university; developed a love of Terrapin athletics while a Boy Scout ushering at Byrd Stadium; UMCP Foundation Board of Trustees.

MARTHA GRIMES, 1954, B.A., ENGLISH; 1955, M.A., ENGLISH
Best-selling author known for her Richard Jury mysteries; *The Anodyne Necklace* won her the 1983 Nero Prize for best American Mystery of the preceding year.

HERBERT A. HAUPTMAN, 1955, PH.D., MATHEMATICS; 1985, HONORARY DOCTORATE
1985 Nobel Laureate in chemistry for the development of direct methods for the determination of crystal structures; only non-chemist to win the award; Alumni Hall of Fame member.

TARA HEISS, 1978, B.S., PHYSICAL EDUCATION
Inducted into the Women's Basketball Hall of Fame in 2003; member of the 1980 team that boycotted the Moscow Olympics; helped the Terrapins reach the championship game of the AIAW Final Four in 1978.

JIM HENSON, 1960, B.S., HOME ECONOMICS; 1978, HONORARY DOCTORATE
Television pioneer, innovator in puppetry, technology and visual arts; creator of Kermit the Frog, Miss Piggy, Big Bird and the Muppets; memorialized in a bronze statue outside the Stamp Student Union; Alumni Hall of Fame member.

JANE HENSON, 1955, B.A., ART EDUCATION
Joint creator of the Muppets with late husband Jim Henson; frequently talks to university students about puppetry.

RICHARD HERMAN, 1967, PH.D., MATHEMATICS
Chancellor of the University of Illinois at Urbana-Champaign; former dean of the College of Computer, Mathematical and Physical Sciences at Maryland.

RAY HIEBERT, 1961, M.A., AMERICAN CIVILIZATION; 1962, M.A., AMERICAN CIVILIZATION
International expert in the growth of modern public relations; founding dean of Maryland's College of Journalism.

BRIAN L. HINMAN, 1982, B.S., ELECTRICAL ENGINEERING
Entrepreneur and industry expert in digital signal processing; holder of 11 U.S. patents; president and CEO of 2Wire; previously founded two other companies, Polycom and PictureTel; UMCP Foundation Board of Trustees.

STENY HOYER, 1963, B.S., GOVERNMENT AND POLITICS; 1988, HONORARY DOCTORATE
Longest-serving member of the U.S. House of Representatives from Southern Maryland in history; House Minority Whip; in 1966, at age 27, won a seat in the Maryland Senate and in 1975 was elected its president, the youngest Senate president in state history; Alumni Hall of Fame member.

HARRY R. HUGHES, 1949, B.S., BUSINESS AND PUBLIC ADMINISTRATION; 1987, HONORARY DOCTORATE
Served two terms as governor of Maryland from 1979–87; his administration began the process of environmentally reclaiming the Chesapeake Bay; Alumni Hall of Fame member.

CARLISLE HUMELSINE, 1937, B.A., EDUCATION/HISTORY
President and chairman of the Colonial Williamsburg Foundation for more than 30 years; almost single-handedly established the field of historic preservation in the United States; Alumni Hall of Fame member.

L. KATE HUTTON, 1973, M.S., ASTRONOMY; 1976, PH.D., ASTRONOMY
World-renowned seismologist at Caltech; known as "The Earthquake Lady" for being the go-to scientist during seismic events.

HUGH NEWELL JACOBSEN, 1951, B.A., FINE ARTS; 1993, HONORARY DOCTORATE
One of the most distinguished architects in North America; has designed hundreds of award-winning buildings, including American embassies in Paris and Moscow; recently designed the university's Samuel Riggs IV Alumni Center; Alumni Hall of Fame member.

FRANKLYN JENIFER, 1970, PH.D., BOTANY
Nationally respected educator; former president of the University of Texas at Dallas and Howard University; former chancellor of higher education in Massachusetts; former vice chancellor of the New Jersey Department of Higher Education.

STAN JONES, 1956, B.S., PHYSICAL EDUCATION
Earned consensus All-America honors with Maryland's 1953 championship football team; 13-year veteran of the NFL; 1991 inductee into the NFL Hall of Fame; 2000 inductee into the College Football Hall of Fame.

CLIFFORD KENDALL, 1954, B.S., FINANCE
American data processing innovator; founder of Computer Data Systems, which provides information technology solutions to government and business; former chair of the Board of Regents.

JAY KERNIS, 1974, B.S., JOURNALISM
Senior vice president for programming with National Public Radio; Emmy Award-winning producer with CBS television for 14 years with a variety of programs, including *60 Minutes* and *CBS This Morning.*

JEONG H. KIM, 1991, PH.D., RELIABILITY ENGINEERING
President of Bell Labs; born in South Korea, immigrated to the United States at age 14; officer on a nuclear submarine; founded Yurie Systems, which became a world leader in advanced data transmission and was bought by Lucent; UMCP Foundation Board of Trustees.

JEFFREY KLUGER, 1976, B.A., GOVERNMENT AND POLITICS
Senior writer for *Time*; co-author of *Lost Moon: The Perilous Voyage of Apollo 13*, upon which the movie *Apollo 13* was based; also a licensed attorney.

Harry Hughes

ALLEN J. KROWE, 1954, B.S., ACCOUNTING; 1994, HONORARY DOCTORATE
Former vice chairman of Texaco; former executive vice president and CFO with IBM; once stole the Navy goat with his Phi Sigma Kappa fraternity brothers.

CHRISTOPHER E. KUBASIK, 1983, B.S., ACCOUNTING
Executive vice president and CFO of Lockheed Martin, one of the largest technology companies in the world; UMCP Foundation Board of Trustees.

ALBIN O. KUHN, 1938, B.S., AGRICULTURAL EDUCATION; 1939, M.S., AGRONOMY; 1948, Ph.D., AGRONOMY
Considered the architect of university expansion in Baltimore; served as vice president of the Baltimore city and county campuses; oversaw the expansion and establishment of UMBC; Alumni Hall of Fame member.

THOMAS LANKFORD, 1969, B.S., AGRICULTURAL ECONOMICS
Former president and COO of SYSCO, a leading foodservice marketer and distributor; began his career in his family's Eastern Shore business, S.E. Lankford, Jr. Produce Company.

JOHN N. LAUER, 1963, B.S., CHEMICAL ENGINEERING
Former president of B.F. Goodrich; retired chairman of Oglebay Norton; honorary citizen of Hungary, named in recognition of his involvement in Hungarian relief and cultural endeavors; UMCP Foundation Board of Trustees.

GEORGE LAURER, 1951, B.S., ELECTRICAL ENGINEERING
Creator of the Universal Product Code system, the 13-line bar code that contains computerized pricing and product information; Alumni Hall of Fame member.

MUNRO LEAF, 1927, B.A., ARTS AND SCIENCES
Author and illustrator of dozens of children's books, including *The Story of Ferdinand*; Alumni Hall of Fame member.

SAMUEL LeFRAK, 1940, B.S., FINANCE; 1990, HONORARY DOCTORATE
Provided affordable urban housing for nearly a half-century; projects included Battery Park City and Gateway Plaza in metropolitan New York; received many awards, including knighthood from Norway and Sweden, the John F. Kennedy Peace Award and honorary doctorates; Alumni Hall of Fame member.

BRIAN LEGETTE, 1989, B.S., ELECTRICAL ENGINEERING
Co-founder of Big Bang Products, now known as 180s LLC, performance gear for cold-weather sports; best known for its hip earwarmers.

LIZ LERMAN, 1970, B.A., DANCE
MacArthur Fellowship ("Genius Award") winner; founding artistic director of the Liz Lerman Dance Exchange for nearly 30 years; dance commissions have included the Kennedy Center, Lincoln Center and BalletMet; Alumni Hall of Fame member.

W.S. LIN, 1978, Ph.D. CANDIDATE, BUSINESS
President of the Tatung Company, a major Taiwanese electronics manufacturer, since 1972; active leader in the Maryland Taiwan Alumni Club.

ROGER C. LIPITZ, 1964, B.S., ACCOUNTING
Co-founded Meridian Healthcare, which became Maryland's largest provider of nursing home and related services; chaired the Baltimore Development Corporation.

JOHN LUCAS, 1976, B.S., BUSINESS ADMINISTRATION
Former All-American and NBA star and coach; also an All-American in tennis and two-time ACC singles and doubles champion.

KATHLEEN MAGEE, 1972, M.Ed., HUMAN DEVELOPMENT EDUCATION
Nurse and clinical social worker; founder of Operation Smile, a nonprofit that performs oral surgeries for children around the world with dental disfigurements; in 1996, helped to open the first burn unit in Nablus, West Bank; Alumni Hall of Fame member.

MARVIN MANDEL, 1939, B.A., ARTS AND HUMANITIES AND LAW; 1969, HONORARY DOCTORATE
Governor of Maryland from 1969–79; longtime member of the University System of Maryland Board of Regents.

MANNING MARABLE, 1976, Ph.D., AMERICAN HISTORY
Professor of public affairs, political science and history at Columbia University; lecturer for the Sing Sing Prison Inmates' master's degree program; writes a nationally syndicated column, "Along the Color Line;" Alumni Hall of Fame member.

RUSSELL E. MARKER, 1923, B.S., CHEMISTRY; 1924, M.S., CHEMISTRY; 1987, HONORARY DOCTORATE
Helped invent the modern octane rating system for gasoline during the 1920s; pioneered the commercial production of cortisone and other steroid drugs; Alumni Hall of Fame member.

TOBIN J. MARKS, 1966, B.S., CHEMISTRY
Vladimir N. Ipatieff Professor of Catalytic Chemistry at Northwestern University; holds nearly 70 patents, many in new plastics development and high-speed data transmission; Alumni Hall of Fame member.

WILLIAM E. MAYER, 1966, B.S., MARKETING; 1967, M.B.A., FINANCE
Chairman of Park Avenue Equity Partners; former dean and professor of the Robert H. Smith School of Business; chair of the Aspen Institute; UMCP Foundation Board of Trustees.

Boomer Esiason

MARK McEWEN, 1972–75
Named one of the country's "Ten Most Trusted TV News Personalities" in 1995; interviewed many prominent newsmakers, including Bill Clinton, Steven Spielberg and Madonna.

GEORGE V. McGOWAN, 1951, B.S., MECHANICAL ENGINEERING; 1997, HONORARY DOCTORATE
Former chairman and CEO of Baltimore Gas and Electric; former chairman of the Board of Regents.

AARON McGRUDER, 1998, B.A., AFRICAN AMERICAN STUDIES
Creator of the popular and edgy comic strip "The Boondocks," which first appeared in *The Diamondback* and now appears daily in more than 250 newspapers.

C. THOMAS McMILLEN, 1974, B.S., CHEMISTRY
Rhodes Scholar; basketball standout at Maryland and in the NBA; U.S. Olympian; three-term U.S. Congressman from Maryland; entrepreneur; UMCP Foundation Board of Trustees.

THOMAS V. "MIKE" MILLER JR., 1964, B.S., MARKETING
Represented Prince George's County in the General Assembly since 1971; became president of the Maryland Senate in 1987; Alumni Hall of Fame member.

PARREN J. MITCHELL, 1952, M.A., SOCIOLOGY
First African American to complete his degree entirely at the College Park campus; first African American elected to U.S. Congress from Maryland; founded and often chaired the Congressional Black Caucus; Alumni Hall of Fame member.

PAUL H. MULLAN, 1968, B.S., MARKETING; 1970, M.B.A., MARKETING
Strategic partner with Charterhouse Group International; former chair of Del Monte Foods; renowned for turning around businesses as diverse as organic food and hula hoops; UMCP Foundation Board of Trustees.

Renaldo Nehemiah

Judith Resnik

RENALDO NEHEMIAH, 1981, B.A., RADIO, TV AND FILM
Set world records in the high hurdles; 1997 inductee into the U.S. Track and Field Hall of Fame; former wide receiver with the NFL's San Francisco 49ers; Alumni Hall of Fame member.

PAUL NORRIS, 1971, M.B.A., MARKETING
Former chairman, president and CEO of W.R. Grace & Co., a global specialty chemicals and materials company; started his career at Grace as a lab technician while in school.

THOMAS R. NORRIS, 1967, B.A., SOCIOLOGY
Navy SEAL in Vietnam; received the Congressional Medal of Honor for rescuing two downed fliers in 1972; retired after 20 years as a special agent with the FBI; Alumni Hall of Fame member.

MICHAEL OLMERT, 1962, B.A., ENGLISH; 1980, PH.D., ENGLISH
Recipient of two Emmy Awards for documentary screenplays on dinosaurs and prehistoric beasts; a lecturer in English at his alma mater; Alumni Hall of Fame member.

PRESTON PADDEN, 1970, B.A., ECONOMICS
Executive vice president for government relations with the Walt Disney Company; former president of ABC Television Network.

ROBERT M. PARKER JR., 1970, B.A., ECONOMICS
Author and publisher of *The Wine Advocate*; one of only a handful of foreigners to receive France's two highest honors; began his professional life as a lawyer.

GEORGE PELECANOS, 1980, B.A., RADIO, TV AND FILM
Author of a dozen crime noir novels set in and around Washington, D.C.; staff writer and story editor for the HBO series, *The Wire.*

STEPHEN PETRANEK, 1970, B.S., JOURNALISM
Editor-in-chief of *Discover* magazine; previously editor-in-chief of *This Old House* and senior editor of *Life*; won the John Hancock financial writing award for a series on stock fraud.

JANE CAHILL PFEIFFER, 1954, B.A., SPEECH; 1979, HONORARY DOCTORATE
First female recipient, in 1966, of a White House Fellowship; had a highly successful 20-year career with IBM and was the company's second female vice president; in 1978, named chairman of the board of NBC; Alumni Hall of Fame member.

ROBERT PINCUS, 1968, B.S., FINANCE
Chairman of Milestone Merchant Partners; former president of BB&T Bank; sponsor of a class of inner-city D.C. schoolchildren; UMCP Foundation Board of Trustees.

KEVIN PLANK, 1997. B.S., BUSINESS ADMINISTRATION
Founder and president of Under Armour; as co-captain of the football team in 1995, came up with the idea for a moisture-wicking compression garment; was named to *Business Week*'s list of top 30-under-30; UMCP Foundation Board of Trustees.

JUDITH RESNIK, 1977, PH.D., ELECTRICAL ENGINEERING
The second American woman in space on the maiden flight of *Discovery* in 1984; perished in the *Challenger* explosion in 1986; also a classical pianist; Alumni Hall of Fame member.

BRENDA BROWN REVER, 1965, B.S., ELEMENTARY EDUCATION
Baltimore civic leader, volunteer and philanthropist; co-chaired the university's *Bold Vision Bright Future* campaign that raised $476 million.

PHILIP R. REVER, 1964, B.S., PERSONNEL
Higher education professional with organizations including ACT, Higher Education Loan Program and Kaludis Consulting; co-chaired the campaign for the Riggs Alumni Center.

PAUL RICHARDS, 1991, M.S., MECHANICAL ENGINEERING
Astronaut for NASA, flew in *Discovery* in 2001; worked on the Hubble Space Telescope at the Goddard Space Flight Center.

SAMUEL RIGGS IV, 1950, B.S., FINANCE
Former chairman and CEO of Sandy Spring National Bank; benefactor of the university's alumni center; a gentleman farmer who raised Angus beef cattle.

MIGUEL RIOS JR., 1972, PH.D., NUCLEAR PHYSICS
Founder and CEO of ORION International Technologies; has been honored as Hispanic Engineer Entrepreneur of the Year and Minority Entrepreneur of the Year.

William P. Cole

HARVEY SANDERS, 1972, B.S., JOURNALISM
Former chairman and CEO of sportswear company Nautica Enterprises; board member of the Boomer Esiason Foundation for Cystic Fibrosis; UMCP Foundation Board of Trustees.

CHUN-SHAN SHEN, 1961, PH.D., PHYSICS
Served as president of his native Taiwan's National Tsing-Hua University; played a major role in building the science and technology infrastructure for Taiwan's modernization; Alumni Hall of Fame member.

DAVID SIMON, 1983, B.G.S., GENERAL STUDIES
Creator and screenwriter of two TV series—*Homicide* and *The Wire*; recipient of two Emmys for the HBO miniseries, *The Corner*; formerly a crime reporter for *The* [Baltimore] *Sun*.

VIVIAN SIMPSON, 1923
First female Secretary of State for Maryland; began her crusade for equal rights for women while at the university; first woman admitted to the Montgomery County bar and elected president of the Montgomery County Bar Association.

WILLIAM WOOLFORD SKINNER, 1895, B.S., AGRICULTURE
Foremost expert in the composition of groundwater in his time; convened a regional committee in 1910 to study the impact of pollution on the Chesapeake Bay and Potomac River; served on the Board of Regents for 18 years, seven as chair; Alumni Hall of Fame member.

HARRY SMITH, 1949, M.S., ELECTRICAL ENGINEERING
Inventor of the pulse Doppler radar; holder of more than a dozen U.S. patents; president of the Westinghouse Defense and Electronic Systems Center in Baltimore for 10 years.

ROBERT H. SMITH, 1950, B.S., ACCOUNTING
Pioneering real estate developer responsible for Crystal City; one of Washington's leading philanthropists; president emeritus of the National Gallery; former chair of Hebrew University; major benefactor, with his wife Clarice, of the university in academics, particularly the business school, and the performing arts; Alumni Hall of Fame member.

ED SNIDER, 1955, B.S., ACCOUNTING
Chairman of Comcast-Spectacor, which owns the Philadelphia Flyers and 76ers; elected to the Hockey Hall of Fame in 1988.

ADELE H. STAMP, 1924, M.A., SOCIOLOGY
Created the position of Dean of Women and held it for 38 years; three-time delegate to the Democratic National Convention; established the university's branch of the American Association of University Women; Alumni Hall of Fame member.

BERT SUGAR, 1957, B.S., BUSINESS AND PUBLIC ADMINISTRATION
Legendary boxing historian; elected to the International Boxing Hall of Fame in 2005; has also written books on baseball and wrestling; acted in *Night and the City* alongside Robert De Niro and *The Great White Hype* with Samuel L. Jackson.

SHIRLEY THOMSON, 1975, M.A., ART
Former director of the Canada Council for the Arts and the National Gallery of Canada; Secretary-General of the Canadian Commission for UNESCO.

REGINALD VAN TRUMP TRUITT, 1914, B.S., BIOLOGICAL SCIENCE; 1922, M.S., BIOLOGICAL SCIENCE
Founder and first director of what became the university's Chesapeake Biological Laboratory at Solomons; led the campaign to designate Assateague Island as a National Seashore; Alumni Hall of Fame member.

MARK TURNER, 1978, B.A., URBAN STUDIES
Entrepreneur; president and co-founder of Steak Escape, purveyor of "America's favorite cheesesteak;" UMCP Foundation Board of Trustees.

JOSEPH TYDINGS, 1951, B.A., ARTS AND HUMANITIES AND LAW
Former U.S. Senator from Maryland; served on the Board of Regents in three decades; stalwart advocate for higher education and public policies; UMCP Foundation Board of Trustees.

MILLARD E. TYDINGS, 1910, B.S., MECHANICAL ENGINEERING; 1933, HONORARY DOCTORATE
Helped create the modern University of Maryland in 1920 when Speaker of the Maryland House of Delegates; served in the U.S. Senate from 1926–50; Alumni Hall of Fame member.

EVELYN PASTEUR VALENTINE, 1976, M.S., FAMILY STUDIES; 1986, PH.D., EDUCATION
Held a variety of roles in Baltimore's public school system; elected 1974 Maryland Teacher of the Year; taught at Loyola and Morgan State; founded the Pasteur Center for Strategic Management; Alumni Hall of Fame member.

LEO VAN MUNCHING, 1950, B.S., MARKETING
Former president of Van Munching & Co., then sole U.S. importer of Heineken and Amstel beers; born in Holland; attended Maryland after serving in World War II; benefactor of the business school.

SCOTT VAN PELT, 1984–90
SportsCenter anchor with ESPN; began broadcasting career as an anchor at the fledgling Golf Channel in 1990; known for touting the Terps on air.

JIM WALTON, 1981, B.A., RADIO, TV AND FILM
President of the CNN News Group; began his career as a video journalist, CNN's entry-level position, a year after CNN was founded; won an Emmy for coverage of the 1996 Olympic Park bombing.

MICHAEL J. WARD, 1972, B.S., MARKETING
Chairman, president and CEO of CSX; has spent entire career in the rail industry; a billiards expert who ran his father's pool hall before getting his M.B.A. from Harvard.

PEDRO WASMER, 1962, B.S., CIVIL ENGINEERING
President and CEO of Somerset Capital Group; company was listed among the 20 fastest-growing Hispanic-owned companies in *Hispanic Business*; native of Cuba; cousin of Lucie Arnaz; UMCP Foundation Board of Trustees.

RANDY WHITE, 1972–74
Former All-Pro lineman for the Dallas Cowboys; inducted into both the College and Pro Football Halls of Fame in 1994.

DEWAYNE WICKHAM, 1974, B.S., JOURNALISM
National columnist for *USA Today* and Gannett News Service; has worked for CBS News, *The* [Baltimore] *Sun*, *U.S. News* and *Black Enterprise*; former president of the National Association of Black Journalists.

DIANNE WIEST, 1965–67
Two-time Oscar winner for Best Supporting Actress in *Hannah and Her Sisters* and *Bullets Over Broadway*; also won an Emmy, two Golden Globes and a Screen Actor's Guild award.

CHARLES "BUCK" WILLIAMS, 1988, B.G.S., GENERAL STUDIES
Seventeen-year veteran of the NBA; NBA Rookie of the Year in 1982; made three All-Star Game appearances; played on the U.S. Olympic team in 1980.

GARY WILLIAMS, 1968, B.S., MARKETING
Head men's basketball coach at Maryland since 1989; led the Terps to their first NCAA national basketball championship in 2002 and the ACC championship in 2004; national and Atlantic Coast Conference Coach of the Year in 2002; Alumni Hall of Fame member.

WALT WILLIAMS, 1992, B.S., MANAGEMENT AND CONSUMER STUDIES
Thirteen-year veteran of the NBA; appeared in 1996 film *Eddie* starring Whoopi Goldberg; established an endowed scholarship fund at Maryland in honor of his late father, Walter Sr.

MORGAN WOOTTEN, 1956, B.S., PHYSICAL EDUCATION
One of the nation's most successful high school basketball coaches during 42 consecutive winning seasons at DeMatha High School in Hyattsville, Md.; inducted into the Basketball Hall of Fame in 2000; Alumni Hall of Fame member.

DENNIS WRAASE, 1966, B.S., ACCOUNTING
President, chairman and CEO of PEPCO Holdings; executive board member for the National Capital Area Council Boy Scouts of America; member of the Financial Executives Institute and the American Institute of Certified Public Accountants.

JAMES A. YORKE, 1966, PH.D., MATHEMATICS
Founder and leader in the field of chaos theory; recipient of the prestigious Japan Prize for his creation of Universal Concepts in Complex Systems; Distinguished University Professor at Maryland.

ERIK YOUNG, 1974, B.S., BIOCHEMISTRY
Physician and real estate developer; president of the Medical Center Development Corporation; UMCP Foundation Board of Trustees.

Chun-Shan Shen

Steny Hoyer

by C.D. Mote Jr.

AT THE BEGINNING, Charles Benedict Calvert founded a small, private agricultural college and proclaimed, "We desire to have an Institution superior to any other." Looking back on this 150-year history, I marvel at how much the University of Maryland has changed, and yet how much it remains the same.

The university is still located on the same beautiful, albeit expanded, grounds that once were a part of Calvert's Riversdale farm. The Rossborough Inn is still here. Mr. Calvert's pride in our heritage and his vision for scholarship and research remain core values. Nevertheless, the spirit of globalization that has gripped the world also shapes our university.

Globalization has connected us all in a new world order where talent and productivity are assembled on a world scale rather than a regional one. Essentially all business is global and so are the world's major problems. Companies once considered American work overseas and foreign-owned companies work in America.

Not surprisingly, the University of Maryland is in tune with these times. Our identity as a marvelously diverse institution that demands excellence in everything it undertakes is widely embraced by our community. Less than three-fifths of our students are from the majority population,

and students come from more than 140 countries. Our student body and faculty demographics mirror the world. Our goal is that every student should have an international experience in this new world. Our university is globalized.

Innovation, entrepreneurship and partnerships on an international scale drive both our world and our university. The search for talent, market and productivity transcends regional, even national boundaries. This is today's world, the world we are preparing our students to live and prosper in. We must ensure that our attention and actions support this global reality while simultaneously serving our state and region.

In 1988 the state of Maryland codified Charles Calvert's vision by mandating in law that our university be ranked among the nation's best public flagships. It went even further in 1999 by stipulating in law that the achievement of this top-tier ranking is the state's first priority in higher education. These remarkable recognitions of the importance of the flagship to the future of the state are singular in the nation.

Equally important to delivering on the state's promise to build a top-ranked flagship university is our promise to deliver simultaneously affordable access to it by the citizens of our state. We are fiercely determined to provide a way for highly talented Maryland students to graduate from the university regardless of financial circumstances.

To deliver these two promises simultaneously, a four-way partnership is required between the university, the state, the University System of Maryland, and our alumni and friends. Each has a key role to play, and only by working together can they deliver the promises. Neither quality nor affordable access can be delivered by any one partner alone. It is a true partnership, and an entrepreneurial and innovative one at that.

Research universities are the most persistent organizations in human history because they represent society's best means for transforming itself. In the decades ahead, our land grant spirit will enable us to capitalize on our strengths in support of our state—we are its most important asset. Charles Benedict Calvert's declaration remains unchanged.

IN 1988 AND AGAIN IN 1999, the General Assembly mandated that the university, as the state's flagship institution, achieve a level of excellence commensurate with the nation's finest universities. Since 1998, Maryland's ranking has moved from 30th to 18th, and in 2005, 32 academic programs ranked in the top 10 nationally. The university ranked 47th globally in 2005 in the Top 500 World Universities, published by the Institute of Higher Education at Shanghai's Jiao Tong University. This recognition reflects the university's expanding role on the international stage. At the same time, the university is committed to building programs of the highest quality while retaining affordable access to students possessed of great talent, but low to moderate financial means, so that they can have the benefit of a University of Maryland degree.

The President's Promise guarantees that every student will have the opportunity to engage in a special, extracurricular learning experience before graduation. A personal international experience that immerses students in a different culture is a primary goal, shaped by a president who has traveled to more than 40 countries.

The $200 million Scholarship Campaign got off to a "hot" start in fall 2004 at a major fund-raising event that transformed the Clarice Smith Performing Arts Center into a Caribbean-themed cruise ship, on which performing arts students entertained the 450 people in attendance. The evening raised more than $1.5 million, capping off a year in which nearly $25 million was committed for scholarships.

The University of Maryland Incentive Awards Program, originally for students from nine Baltimore City public high schools who have overcome great disadvantage to enroll in college, expanded into Prince George's County and will include freshmen from that county entering in fall 2006. The inaugural class of Incentive Award Scholars, who began their undergraduate journey in fall 2001, are shown below.

IN ADDITION TO TRADITIONAL
EDUCATION, research and service, students
and faculty are encouraged to learn about
commercializing their concepts and the results of
their research. The knowledge economy will really
take off when students and faculty plan to spin
off their ideas into the marketplace and obstacles
to try so are few. In order to increase the impact
of the entrepreneurial programs and activities
in engineering, business and other units of the
university that contribute to commercialization
and economic development, the university has
formed a network of entrepreneurs to foster
cooperation and to provide resource development,
coordination and collaboration. It's yet one more
way that the university reinforces its integral role
in the state's economy.

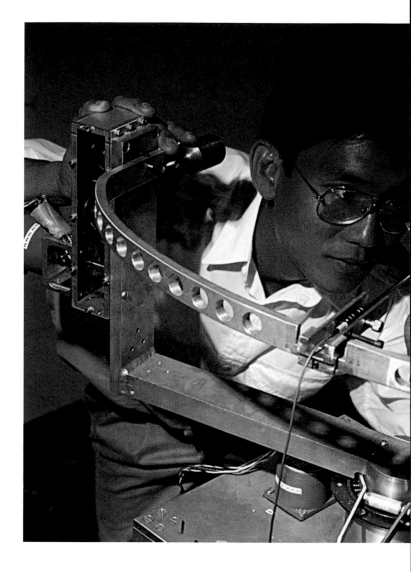

*President C.D. Mote Jr. presides over the
groundbreaking at the College of Chemical and Life
Sciences' Bioscience Research Building in September
2004. Scheduled for completion in the fall of 2006,
the building will house research space for as many
as three dozen scientists and laboratories devoted
to three high-impact areas of the biosciences: host-
pathogen interactions, comparative and functional
genomics, and sensory neuroscience.*

An undergraduate student prepares for a career in the 21st-century field of bioscience. President Mote has made the biosciences a vital component of his plan to grow the university's traditional strengths. "Strength in biosciences is the key to the future of the state's economy," Mote recently told the General Assembly, "key to the future of the university, and key to the faculty's ability to capture a share of the huge amount of federal funding pouring into biosciences."

*M Square One will be
completed in fall 2006.
Its tenants will include
the National Oceanic and
Atmospheric Administration,
research teams like the
Earth System Modeling
collaborations, private sector
firms who want to be close
to the university and other
like-minded tenants.*

PARTNERSHIPS WITH ENTITIES outside the university, such as with national laboratories, are a natural effort to take advantage of the university's location. To facilitate such partnerships, the university has created the 124-acre M Square, University of Maryland Research Park, which will be the largest such facility in the state of Maryland and the greater Washington, D.C., metropolitan area when fully developed. The outcomes of such industrial partnerships include engagement on current problems facing a major U.S. corporation, growth in opportunities for students, faculty and visitors, support for students through internships and employment and support for faculty and postdoctoral scholars for new areas of targeted basic and applied research.

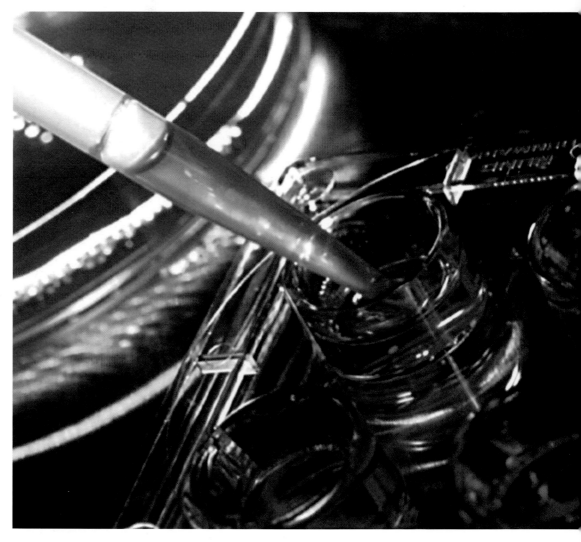

The Center for the Advanced Study of Language (CASL) is the national laboratory for advanced research and development on language and national security and the largest language research facility in the country. Such issues as how stress and fatigue can impair federal workers' foreign language competency, challenges and techniques for acquiring very high level language capabilities, mastering multiple Arabic dialects and pre-deployment language/culture training for the military are some aspects under study.

With concerns about emerging infectious diseases— either naturally occurring or as a result of terrorist threats—the increasing subject of public policy debates, the university began developing plans to create a school of public health in partnership with the University of Maryland, Baltimore.

EXPANDING TIES GLOBALLY is essential for both businesses and universities. In part that will include a broadening of what is meant by education, to think beyond traditional degree programs. This is already beginning to happen. The Institute for Global Chinese Affairs has provided 1,000 Chinese executives with a one-month to one-year certificate experience at the university. The Robert H. Smith School of Business offers degree, custom and certification programs in learning locations on four continents including Asia, North America, Europe and Africa.

President Mote confers with government and academic leaders to strengthen the university's ties globally. Here he meets with Daniel Scioli, vice president of Argentina.

Recently, the university cemented a partnership with China's pre-eminent Peking University and other institutions to bolster joint projects involving business; chemical and life sciences; computer, mathematical and physical sciences; and behavioral and social sciences.

President Mote introduced Nelson Mandela when the former president of South Africa appeared on campus to present the 2001 Sadat Lecture for Peace.

President Mote speaks on the role of universities in this age of globalization in his travels throughout the world, such as at National Central University in Taiwan, where he addressed an audience of university officials, government leaders and CEOs of corporations. He has also given talks on this theme in China and, most recently, Egypt, emphasizing the need for universities to forge partnerships with other universities and governments.

Acknowledgments

PROJECT TEAM: Dianne T. Burch, University Editor; John T. Consoli, University Photographer; Anne S.K. Turkos, University Archivist

ESSAYISTS: Prologue, Ira Berlin; Chapter 2, Irwin L. Goldstein; Chapter 3, J. Robert Dorfman; Chapter 4, Leonard J. Elmore, Esq.; Chapter 5, Virginia W. Beauchamp; Chapter 6, David C. Driskell; Chapter 7, Brenda Brown Rever; Chapter 9, C.D. Mote Jr.

ANNIVERSARY LEADERSHIP: James F. Harris, chair, 150th Anniversary Planning Committee; Teresa Flannery, Assistant Vice President for Marketing and Communications; Barbara C. Quinn, Executive Director, University Relations; Brodie Remington, Vice President for University Relations

FACULTY CONSULTANTS: Chair, Andrea Hill Levy, Associate Vice President, Academic Affairs; members, Cordell W. Black, Associate Provost for Faculty Affairs; George E. Dieter, Glenn L. Martin Professor, Engineering; David S. Falk, Professor Emeritus, Physics and Assistant Vice President (retired); Martin O. Heisler, Professor, Government and Politics; Claire G. Moses, Professor, Women's Studies; Phyllis Moser-Veillon, Professor Emerita, Nutrition and Food Science

WRITER: Bill Beck, Lakeside Writers' Group

BOOK DESIGN: Jennifer Paul, Jennifer Paul Design

BOOK LAYOUT: Amanda D. Guilmain, Donning Company Publishers

RESEARCH SUPPORT: Robert Headley and Elizabeth McAllister, University Archives; Marc W. Jaffe, Office of University Relations; Juan Manuel Ramirez, Office of University Publications; Rhonda Malone and Ellin K. Scholnick, Office of Academic Affairs

REVIEW SUPPORT: Ruth M. Alvarez, Literary Manuscripts, University of Maryland Libraries; Pamela Koch, Donning Company Publishers; Kimberly Marselas and Tom Ventsias, Office of University Publications; Pamela Stone, Office of the Vice President, University Relations

PICTORIAL TIMELINE PHOTO CREDITS:

Opening page, John T. Consoli

1856—Stock Certificate, Maryland Manuscripts Collection

1862, 1891, 1922 and 1923—Historical Manuscripts

1858—Charles Benedict Calvert—Library of Congress Prints and Photographs Division, LC-DIG-cwpbh-03464

1859, 1865, 1874, 1888, 1892, 1894, 1898, 1912, 1914, 1915, 1916, 1928, both 1932, 1933, 1946, 1951, 1953, 1955, 1957, 1958, 1963, 1977 and 1986—University Archives

1964, 1965, 1976, 1985, 1989, 1994, 1999 (Maryland Day), 2005 (Jeong H. Kim Engineering Building)—John T. Consoli

1982—Bill Denison

1969, 1987 and 2002—Athletic Media Relations

1999—portrait of C.D. Mote Jr., Jeremy Green

2005—Samuel Riggs IV Alumni Center, Michael Morgan

PHOTO CREDITS:

Athletic Media Relations: p. 62, top right; pp. 98–99; p. 101, top; p. 102, bottom; p. 114; p. 115, left

Baltimore News American, Special Collections, University of Maryland Libraries, p. 27, left, top and bottom

Campus Photographic Services, p. 30

College Park Airport Museum, Brinckerhoff Collection, Front Endpaper

John T. Consoli: Front Cover; Back Cover, top left and bottom right; pp. 2–3; p. 4 (left); p. 5; p. 6; p. 20; p. 28, right; p. 29, bottom; p. 31, top; pp. 32–37; p. 40, bottom; pp. 43–44; p. 46, bottom; p. 47–49; p. 55; p. 58, left; p. 59, bottom; p. 60, top; p. 63, top and bottom, left; p. 68, left and top right; p. 69; p. 70, top; p. 71, bottom; pp. 72–73, bottom; p. 74, right; p. 75–76; p. 77, bottom; p. 78; p. 79, middle and bottom; p. 81, top; pp. 82–83; pp. 84–85, top; p. 86; p. 87, bottom; pp. 88–90; p. 92; pp. 94–95; p. 97, bottom; p. 100; p. 101, bottom; p. 103, bottom; p. 108, bottom; p. 109, top; pp. 120–123; p. 125; Back Endpaper

Courtesy of: NASA, p. 40, top; James Yorke, p. 40, center; p. 57, bottom right; Kenneth Holum, p. 74, left; College Park Scholars, p. 77, middle; Parren T. Mitchell, p. 111, left; CBS, p. 111, right; Mary

Stallings Coleman, p. 112, left; Henson Productions, p. 112, right; Harry R. Hughes, p. 113, bottom; Chun-Shan Shen, p. 117, top; Steny Hoyer, p. 117, bottom; NOAA, p. 124, top; CASL, p. 124, bottom; Saul Sosnowski, p. 126, top and bottom right; p. 127, bottom.

Al Danegger, p. 42, bottom

Cameron Davidson, pp. 84–85, bottom

Amy Davis, p. 46, top

Bill Denison, p. 72, top

Raymond Dilzer, p. 91, bottom

Glen Dimock, pp. 118–119

Larry French, p. 63, bottom right

Mark Gail, p. 108, top

Jeremy Green, p. 93

Lisa Helfert, p. 106, top

Historical Manuscripts, University of Maryland Libraries: p. 11, top left; p. 16, top left; p. 19; pp. 22–23; p. 24; p. 25, top; p. 39, bottom; p. 45, bottom; p. 54, top

Michael Morgan: p. 41; p. 79, top; p. 96; p. 104; p. 127, top

Mac Nelson, p. 66

Mark Nystrom: p. 87, top; pp. 88–89; p. 101, center

Edwin Remsberg, p. 38

Kenneth Rubin, p. 102, top

Smithsonian Institution Archives, Record Unit 95, Box 27B, Negative #SA-606, p. 39, top right

Stan Stearns, p. 28, left

Scott Suchman: Back Cover, middle bottom; p. 4, right; p. 73, top; p. 77, top; p. 91, top; p. 105, bottom; p. 126, left

University Archives: Back Cover, top right and bottom left; pp. 8–9; p. 10; p. 11, bottom; pp. 12–15; p. 16, bottom; p. 17–18; p. 25, bottom; p. 26; p. 27, far right; p. 29, top right; p. 30, basketball; p. 31, bottom; p. 42, top; p. 45, top; pp. 50–53; p. 54, bottom; p. 56; p. 57, top; p. 58, top and bottom, left; p. 59, top; p. 60, bottom right; p. 61, middle and bottom; p. 62, bottom; p. 64; p. 68, bottom right; p. 71, bottom; p. 80; p. 103, top, center and right; pp. 104–105, top; p. 106, top right and bottom; p. 107; p. 108, top left; p. 110; p. 115, right; p. 116

Bill Weems: p. 60, bottom left; p. 61, top right; p. 62, top left; p. 65; p. 97, top; p. 109, bottom